PROCESS CONSULTATION: ITS ROLE
IN ORGANIZATION DEVELOPMENT

EDGAR H. SCHEIN

Massachusetts Institute of Technology

ADDISON-WESLEY PUBLISHING COMPANY
Reading, Massachusetts · Menlo Park, California
London · Amsterdam · Don Mills, Ontario · Sydney

This book is in the Addison-Wesley series:

ORGANIZATION DEVELOPMENT

Editors
Edgar Schein
Warren Bennis
Richard Beckhard

ISBN 0-201-06733-1
MNOPQRST-CO-79876

FOREWORD

The purpose of this common foreword to all the volumes of the Addison-Wesley Series on Organization Development is twofold: (1) to give the reader some idea as to the origin and purpose of the series; and (2) to guide the reader through the content of the different books.

The series came to be because we felt there was a growing theory and practice of something called "organization development," but most students, colleagues, and managers knew relatively little about it. Many of us are highly active as O.D. consultants, but little has been written about what we do when we are with a client or what our underlying theory of consultation is. We were also acutely aware of the fact that, though there are common assumptions shared by most practitioners of O.D., there are great individual variations in the strategies and tactics employed by different consultants. The field is still emerging and new methods are constantly being invented. It seemed appropriate, therefore, not to try to write a single text, but to give several of the foremost theorist-practitioners a chance to explain their own view of O.D. and their own style of working with client systems.

The authors of this series of six books represent a variety of points of view, but they do not exhaust the major approaches currently in use in O.D. There are some obvious names missing—Argyris, Tannenbaum, Ferguson, Bradford, Davis, Burke—to name just a few. We hope in future volumes of the series to get these men and others to write about their theory and practice.

The six books of this series can be described as follows: Bennis presents a very broad survey of the history and present practice of O.D. How and why did it come about, what is it, and what are some of the major unresolved issues in O.D.? The Beckhard volume is a systematic attempt to describe the various strategies and tactics employed in different kinds of O.D. efforts. Beckhard goes beyond his own approach and tries to build a general framework within which most O.D. programs can be located. The Beckhard and Bennis volumes together give the reader an excellent overview of the field.

The two volumes by Blake and Mouton and by Lawrence and Lorsch are somewhat more personalized statements of their particular views of how organizations function, how organizational excellence is to be judged, and how an O.D. effort can contribute to the achievement of such excellence. Both books focus on total organization systems and attempt to show how intervention in organizations leads to constructive change and development.

The volumes by Walton and Schein are written at a more specific level. They highlight some of the day-to-day activities of the consultant as he works with a client system in the context of an O.D. program. Both deal with the process of the consultation itself. In the Walton book the focus is on the process by which the consultant uses himself to aid in the resolution of conflict. In the Schein book the idea of "process consultation" is introduced and explained in detail. The kinds of organizational processes which are described in these last two volumes lie at the heart of O.D. efforts, but the focus of the books is on the moment-to-moment behavior of the consultant rather than the overall design of the O.D. program.

The six books were written independently with only broad guidelines and minimum coordination by the editors. It was our hope and intention to get six very personal and unique statements, rather than a closely integrated set of "chapters." We feel the amount of overlap is minimal, and that the books in fact complement each other very well in being written at different levels of generality. We hope that the reader will sense that the field of O.D. is converging toward common theories and practices, but that we are a long way from being able to produce a definitive "text" on the subject.

March 1969.

Edgar H. Schein
Richard Beckhard
Warren G. Bennis

PREFACE

This short book on Process Consultation had, in retrospect, a long history. I think it all began in the late 1950's when I became exposed to Doug McGregor. I knew that Doug was an active and successful consultant, and I learned that Doug wanted his colleagues to share in the excitement which the consultation process brought with it. In his lectures he often spoke of experiences with companies, and, whenever possible, he created opportunities for me and others to learn the art of influencing organizations through some direct intervention.

I remember clearly a frustration I had in listening to Doug. He could communicate the excitement of consultation, but he could never quite articulate just what he personally did when he operated as a consultant. I always felt that the inability to write about such actions in a concrete manner was unfortunate in that it deprived others of important insights. I think I resolved at that time to write about my own consultation experiences, if and when I could.

For the next five to ten years I was unable to act on my resolution. What brought me back to life was a sharp goad from Charles Savage who was visiting the Sloan School in 1967-68. He demanded to know in a friendly but firm way why I was "wasting my time teaching a few managers a little psychology when I could be writing up research results which would influence thousands?" This question so upset me that I went home and promptly wrote a ten-page paper on what my consultation experiences really were, why I did not think that I was just "teaching a little psychology to a few managers," and how research and theory interlocked with consultation. This book is essentially an elaboration of that ten-page paper, and I will forever be grateful to Charlie Savage for providing the impetus to get it out of my system.

My intentions are twofold: (1) to present the reader with those ideas from social psychology which I have found most useful in my consultation experiences; and (2) to give a personal and detailed statement of what I do when I consult. I am not trying to build a new theory or to document a position with research findings. My goals are more personal, and I suspect the reader will find his own evidence that, like any human being, I lack self-insight in certain crucial areas. If such lack of insight has led me into inconsistencies or fallacies in logic, I beg the reader's indulgence. Perhaps this book will lead others to point out these flaws and to expose their own theories and practice, thus moving the whole enterprise of consultation and organization development a step forward.

I am most grateful to my various clients for the challenge, excitement, and fun they have provided me by letting me help them with their various organizational and interpersonal dilemmas. To preserve their privacy I cannot name them individually, but I thank them collectively. The examples I present in my text are deliberately chosen to be a *mixture* of experiences drawn from various private and public organizations. The anonymity of each client is thus preserved, but I have reported the essence of the experiences as faithfully as I am able.

I am also grateful to my colleagues from whom I have learned much about the art of consultation—particularly Richard Beckhard, Warren Bennis, and Chris Argyris. The field of consultation requires constant innovation, and these men have been a never-ending source of new ideas and new practices.

My wife deserves thanks, as usual, for providing the supportive home climate which made it possible to think and write. Finally, I would like to thank my secretary, Linda Whitehead, for her efforts in typing, organizing, and generally supervising the difficult chore of producing, the final manuscript.

Cambridge, Mass.   Edgar H. Schein
January 1969

CONTENTS

PART 1
DIAGNOSIS

Part 1 of this book describes in considerable detail the human processes in organizations, in order to bring out the kinds of things the process consultant focuses on when he attempts to understand what is going on in the organization. In Part 2 we will shift the focus of analysis away from diagnosis toward the kinds of intervention which the process consultant makes. Without an understanding of the *diagnostic* process, however, these interventions will not make sense. Therefore, the reader who is not familiar with interpersonal and group theory should first read Part 1. On the other hand, the reader who is familiar with concepts of communication, group process, leadership, and the like, can skip immediately to Part 2.

1
INTRODUCTION

This book is about a special kind of consultation which I am calling *Process Consultation* (P-C)—what it is, and what role it plays in organizational development (OD).

In focusing upon process consultation I will be looking at one of the key activities which goes on at the beginning of (and throughout) any OD effort. OD is a planned organization-wide kind of program, but its component parts are usually activities which the consultant carries out with individuals or small groups. This volume will focus on these kinds of activities and therefore will deal primarily with *interpersonal* and *group* events. I will not try to give an overview of OD programs as a whole, but will focus on the process by which the consultant builds readiness for OD programs, actually conducts training as part of the OD effort, and works with the key individuals of an organization as part of an OD program.

The field of consultation has grown remarkably in recent years, yet surprisingly little has been written about it. What does a consultant do for an organization and how does he do it? Does he provide expert information, help to diagnose complex problems, give managers support and comfort, listen and provide counsel, solve organizational problems, help managers to implement difficult or unpopular decisions, or some or all of these?

Seymour Tilles has stated in his analysis of the consultation process that unless the manager knows what he is looking for in a consulting relationship, he is likely to be sorely disappointed (Tilles, 1961). The

3

manager's real problem, however, often is that he *does not know* what he is looking for, and, indeed should not really be expected to know. All he knows is that something is not right. An important part of the consultation process is to help the manager or the organization define what the problem is, and only then, decide what further kind of help is needed.

Managers often sense that all is not well or that things could be better, and yet do not have the tools with which to translate their vague feelings into concrete action steps. The kind of consultation I will attempt to describe in this book deals with problems of this sort. Process consultation does not assume that the manager or the organization knows what is wrong, or what is needed, or what the consultant should do. All that is required for the process to begin constructively is some *intent* on the part of someone in the organization to improve the way things are going. The consultation process itself then helps the manager to define diagnostic steps which lead ultimately to action programs or concrete changes.

Process consultation is a difficult concept to describe simply and clearly. It does not lend itself to a simple definition to be followed by a few illustrations. Instead, I will try first to give some perspective by contrasting P-C with more traditional consultation models. Then I will provide some historical perspective, to indicate why P-C is an increasingly relevant activity in today's organizational world and why it is particularly relevant to OD efforts. Finally, I will devote the bulk of this volume to the actual procedure of P-C: what the consultant looks for, how the process starts, how a relationship is developed with the client, what kinds of interventions are made, how the process is evaluated, and how it is terminated.

In discussing each of these topics, I will draw as much as possible on concrete examples from my own experience, and will try to highlight the assumptions the consultant makes, the criteria by which he decides to choose various alternatives available to him, and the kinds of dilemma he faces in trying to be maximally helpful to the organization.

HOW IS PROCESS CONSULTATION
DIFFERENT FROM OTHER CONSULTATION?

We do not have in the field of management a neat typology of consultation processes, but a few models can be identified from the literature (e.g. Tilles, 1961; Argyris, 1961; Daccord, 1967) and from my own experience in watching consultants work.

The Purchase Model

The most prevalent model of consultation is certainly the "purchase of expert information or an expert service." The buyer, an individual manager or some group in the organization, defines a need—something he wishes to know or some activity he wishes carried out—and, if he doesn't feel the organization itself has the time or capability, he will look to a consultant to fill the need. For example: (1) A manager may wish to know how a particular group of consumers feel, or how to design a plant efficiently, or how to design an accounting system which fully utilizes a computer's capability. (2) The manager may wish to find out how he could more effectively organize some group. This would require some surveying of their activities, attitudes, and work habits. (3) A manager may wish to institute a morale survey procedure for his production units, or an analysis of the quality of some complex product. In the first of the above examples, the manager desires *information;* in the latter two examples, he wishes to *purchase a service* from the consultant. In each of these cases there is an assumption that the manager knows what kind of information or what kind of service he is looking for. The success of the consultation then depends upon:

1. whether the manager has correctly diagnosed his own needs;

2. whether he has correctly communicated these needs to the consultant;

3. whether he has accurately assessed the capability of the consultant to provide the right kind of information or service; and

4. whether he has thought through the consequences of having the consultant gather information, and/or the consequences of implementing changes which may be recommended by the consultant.

The frequent dissatisfaction voiced by managers with the quality of the services they feel they receive from their consultants is easily explainable when one considers how many things have to go right for the purchase model to work.

Process consultation, in contrast, involves the manager and the consultant in a period of *joint* diagnosis. The process consultant is willing to come into an organization without a clear mission or clear need, because of an underlying assumption that most organizations could probably be more effective than they are if they could identify what processes (work flow, interpersonal relations, communications, intergroup relations, etc.) need improvement. A closely related assumption is that no organizational form is perfect, that every organizational form has strengths and weaknesses. The process consultant would urge any manager with whom he is working not to leap into an action program, particularly if it involves any kind of changes in organizational structure, until the organization itself has done a thorough diagnosis and assessment of the strengths and weaknesses of the present structure.

The importance of *joint* diagnosis derives from the fact that the consultant can seldom learn enough about the organization to really know what a better course of action would be for that *particular group* of people with their *particular sets* of traditions, styles, and personalities. However, the consultant can help the manager to become a sufficiently good diagnostician himself, and can provide enough alternatives, to enable the manager to solve the problem. This last point highlights another assumption underlying P-C: problems will stay solved longer and be solved more effectively if the organization solves its own problems; the consultant has a role in teaching diagnostic and problem-solving skills, but he should not work on the actual concrete problem himself.

The Doctor-Patient Model

Another traditionally popular model of consultation is that of doctor-patient. One or more executives in the organization decide to bring in a consultant or team of consultants to "look them over," much as a patient might go to his doctor for an annual physical. The consultants are supposed to find out what is wrong with which part of the organization, and then, like a physician, recommend a program of therapy. Often the manager singles out some unit of the organization where he is having difficulty or where performance has fallen off, and asks the consultant to determine "what is wrong with our —— department."

As most readers will recognize from their own experience, in spite of the popularity of this model it is fraught with difficulties. One of the most obvious difficulties is that the organizational unit which is defined as the patient may be reluctant to reveal the kinds of information which the consultant is likely to need in order to make his diagnosis. In fact, it is quite predictable that on questionnaires and in interviews systematic distortions will occur. The direction of distortion will depend upon the company climate. If the climate is one of mistrust and insecurity, the respondent is likely to hide any damaging information from the consultant because he fears that his boss will punish him for revealing problems; if the climate is one of high trust, the respondent is likely to view contact with the consultant as an opportunity to gripe, leading to exaggeration of problems. Unless the consultant spends considerable time *observing* the department, he is not likely to get an accurate picture.

An equally great difficulty in the doctor-patient model is that the patient is sometimes unwilling to believe the diagnosis or accept the prescription offered by the consultant. I suspect most companies have drawers full of reports by consultants, each loaded with diagnoses and recommendations which are either not understood or not accepted by the "patient." What is wrong, of course, is that the doctor, the consultant, has not built up a common diagnostic frame of reference with the patient, his client. If the consultant does all the diagnosis while the client-manager waits passively for a prescription, it is predictable that a communication gulf will arise which will make the prescription seem irrelevant and/or unpalatable.

Process consultation, in contrast, focuses on joint diagnosis and the passing on to the client of diagnostic skills. The consultant may recognize early in his work what some of the problems are in the organization and how they might be solved. He does not advance them prematurely, however, for two reasons. One, he may be wrong and may damage his relationship with the client by a hasty diagnosis which turns out to be wrong. Two, he recognizes that even if he is right, the client is likely to be defensive, to not listen to the diagnosis, to misunderstand what the consultant is saying, and to argue with it.

It is a key assumption underlying P-C that the client must learn to see the problem for himself, to share in the diagnosis, and to be *actively involved* in generating a remedy. The process consultant may play a key role in helping to sharpen the diagnosis and in providing alternative remedies which may not have occurred to the client. But he encourages the client to make the ultimate decision as to what remedy to apply. Again, the consultant does this on the assumption that if he teaches the client to diagnose and remedy situations, problems will be solved more permanently and the client will be able to solve new problems as they arise.

It should be emphasized that the process consultant may or may not be expert in solving the particular problem which is uncovered. The important point in P-C is that such expertise is less relevant than are the skills of involving the client in self-diagnosis and helping him to find a remedy which fits his particular situation and his unique set of needs. The process consultant must be an expert in how to diagnose and how to develop a helping relationship. He does not need to be an expert on production, marketing, finance, and the like. If problems are uncovered in specific areas like these, the process consultant would help the client to find an expert resource in those areas, but he would *also* help the client to think through how best to get help from such an expert.

ASSUMPTIONS UNDERLYING PROCESS CONSULTATION

Let me pull together here the assumptions stated thus far. I have said that P-C assumes that:

1. Managers often do not know what is wrong and need special help in diagnosing what their problems actually are.

2. Managers often do not know what kinds of help consultants can give to them; they need to be helped to know what kind of help to seek.

3. Most managers have a constructive intent to improve things but need help in identifying what to improve and how to improve it.

4. Most organizations can be more effective if they learn to diagnose their own strengths and weaknesses. No organizational form is perfect; hence every form of organization will have some weaknesses for which compensatory mechanisms need to be found.

5. A consultant could probably not, without exhaustive and time-consuming study, learn enough about the culture of the organization to suggest reliable new courses of action. Therefore, he must work jointly with members of the organization who *do* know the culture intimately from having lived within it.

6. The client must learn to see the problem for himself, to share in the diagnosis, and to be actively involved in generating a remedy. One of the process consultant's roles is to provide new and challenging alternatives for the client to consider. Decision-making about these alternatives must, however, remain in the hands of the client.

7. It is of prime importance that the process consultant be expert in how to *diagnose* and how to *establish effective helping relationships* with clients. Effective P-C involves the passing on of both these skills.

DEFINITION OF PROCESS CONSULTATION

With these assumptions in mind, we can attempt to formulate a more precise definition of P-C.

P-C is a set of activities on the part of the consultant which help the client to perceive, understand, and act upon process events which occur in the client's environment.

The process consultant seeks to give the client "insight" into what is going on around him, within him, and between him and other people. The events to be observed and learned from are primarily the various human actions which occur in the normal flow of work, in the conduct of meetings, and in formal or informal encounters between members of the organization. Of particular relevance are the client's own actions and their impact on other people.

It should be noted that this definition brings in several new concepts and assumptions, relating in general to what one looks for in making one's *diagnosis*. The important elements to study in an organization are the human processes which occur. A good diagnosis of an organizational problem may go beyond an analysis of such processes but it cannot afford to ignore them. By implication, the process consultant is primarily an expert on processes at the individual, interpersonal, and intergroup levels. His expertise may go beyond these areas, but it must at the minimum include them. Improvement in organizational effectiveness will occur through effective problem finding in the human process area, which in turn will depend upon the ability of managers to learn diagnostic skills through exposure to P-C.

I am not contending that focusing on human processes is the *only* path to increasing organizational effectiveness. Obviously there is room in most organizations for improved production, financial, marketing, and other processes. I am arguing, however, that the various functions which make up an organization are always mediated by the interactions of people, so that the organization can never escape its human processes (Schein, 1965). As long as organizations are networks of people, there will be processes occurring between them. Therefore, it is obvious that the better understood and better diagnosed these processes are, the greater will be the chances of finding solutions to technical problems which will be accepted and used by the members of the organization.

2

HUMAN PROCESSES IN ORGANIZATIONS: AN OVERVIEW

In my book *Organizational Psychology* (1965), I stated that a new field typically develops around a set of new concepts combined with some techniques for studying these concepts. Thus organizations became a focus of inquiry for psychologists as tools were developed for studying organizations. A similar argument can be made for the study of human processes in organization—it has developed in direct relation to our ability to observe and do research on individual, interpersonal, and intergroup phenomena.

STRUCTURE *VS.* PROCESS

Early studies of organization were dominated by the "scientific management" school of thought leading to an almost exclusive preoccupation with the "structural" or static elements of organization: What is the correct division of labor? Who should have which responsibilities? Should the production department report directly to the president or through a product organization involving other functions? What is the right span of control? How many levels should there be in the hierarchy? and so on. This concern for organizational statics is understandable and appropriate because organizations are open systems which exist in an uncertain environment. In order to survive as organizations they must conserve stability in the face of recurring disintegrative pressures from the environment. Just as total societies develop a social structure, laws, traditions, and culture as a way of stabilizing themselves, so organizations develop and must conserve their structures and culture.

The appeal of the structural approach can readily be seen in the field of consultation. Management consulting firms are often brought in to examine the existing management *structure* and to recommend alternate forms which are presumed to be more effective for achieving organizational goals (Daniel, 1966). If the recommendations are acted upon, reporting relations are likely to be changed, departments are likely to be phased out or moved, and other similar drastic alterations made. The personalities of individual managers are taken into account in the diagnostic process, but these also tend to be viewed structurally as static factors to be considered in designing the new structure.

The problem with this approach is not that it is wrong but that it is incomplete. The network of positions and roles which define the formal organizational structure is occupied by people, and those people in varying degrees put their own personalities into getting their job done. The effect of this is not only that each role occupant has a certain style of doing his work, but that he has certain patterns of relating to other people in the organization. These patterns become structured, and out of such patterns arise traditions which govern the way members of the organization relate to each other.

Such traditions cannot be inferred or deciphered from knowing only the formal organizational relations; it is therefore doubtful that they can be changed by changing only the formal structure. I believe that the consultant must also examine the *processes* which occur between people as a way of understanding the informal relationships, the traditions, and the culture which surrounds the structure.

To put the issue another way, the roles which people occupy partly determine how they will behave. It is important to have the right structure of roles for effective organizational performance, but at the same time, people's personalities, perceptions, and experiences also determine how they will behave in their roles and how they will relate to others.

Only if these relationships among the role occupants are working smoothly can organizational effectiveness be ensured. If the consultant is interested in organization improvement, he must therefore study the processes which occur between people and groups.

SOME HISTORICAL ROOTS OF PROCESS CONSULTATION

The study of organizational processes has several historical roots. One of these roots is the field of group dynamics as developed originally under the leadership of Kurt Lewin. A second root was the development of techniques of studying group process, such as those developed by Chapple (1940) in anthropology, Bales (1950) in sociology, and Carter *et al.* (1951) in psychology.

The classical experiments by White and Lippitt (1953) on the effects of different kinds of leadership showed that group productivity and morale were very much affected by the leadership *style* of the formal leader. Bales (1950) in his extensive and detailed analyses of small-group problem-solving showed that groups developed certain patterns of behavior which were quite predictable. For example, two kinds of leader tended to emerge: a task leader, who helps the group do its job, and a "socio-emotional" leader, who helps maintain good relations among members. Only rarely were these two leaders the same person in the groups studied. Clearly it was possible to study the process events occurring in a group in a reliable manner, and clearly this paid off in finding nonobvious regularities in such behavior.

A third, and closely related, historical root was the development of group-dynamics training methods associated with the National Training Laboratories (Bradford *et al.*, 1965; Schein and Bennis, 1965). Deriving from Lewinian concepts of action-research, a technology of group observation and intervention in group processes has been developed over the last twenty years. This approach represents the most important historical precursor to P-C, in that most of the assumptions which P-C makes in relation to working with an organization are derived of assumptions which "trainers" make in working with laboratory-training groups. For example, the trainer sees himself not as a teacher or an expert, but as someone who helps group members to discover what kinds of events are occurring in the group and what effects such events are having on themselves and other members.

A fourth root is the study of group relations and interpersonal processes in industrial organizations. Originating in the work of Mayo, Roethlisberger, and Dickson, carried forward by Arensberg, Whyte, Homans, and others who studied the "informal" organization in industry, and taken to the management ranks in works such as Melville Dalton's (1959), these studies showed that how people actually relate to each other bears only a limited relation to how the formal organizational structure says they should behave. These studies, more than any others, illustrate the need to study human processes in organizations by actual observation rather than to accept at face value what people say in interviews or on questionnaires.

Finally, an important root has been the work of Muzapher Sherif (1961) who showed that regularities could be demonstrated not only within small groups but also between groups, and thus opened up the whole area of intergroup relations. For example, the behavior and feelings of people when they are in intergroup win-lose competition are sufficiently regular and predictable that one can readily create laboratory demonstrations from the original experiments (Blake and Mouton, 1961).

As can be seen, process consultation is anchored deeply in social psychology, sociology, and anthropology. Good diagnosis of the sort which P-C calls for, therefore, cannot be achieved without a working knowledge of what these disciplines have contributed to the understanding of organizational phenomena. The understanding and analysis of human processes in organizations requires not merely an attitude or a decision to focus on such processes, but also a good deal of technical skill and a knowledge of what to look for, how to look for it, and how to interpret it. Helping an organization to do its own diagnosis and to solve its own problems requires additional skills which are derived primarily from laboratory-training experience and actual consultation experience.

TYPES OF HUMAN PROCESSES IN ORGANIZATIONS

So far I have been speaking of human processes in organizations only in general terms. What specifically are such processes and how do they relate to OD? In the next six chapters I will describe in detail those kinds of processes which I consider to be most crucial for effective organization performance: (1) communication; (2) member roles and functions in groups; (3) group problem-solving and decision-making; (4) group norms and group growth; (5) leadership and authority; and (6) intergroup cooperation and competition.

The processes to be described are not intended to be an exhaustive treatment of interpersonal, group, and organizational process. Instead, I have tried to select those processes to which I find myself most often directing my efforts when I am in the consultant role. Also, I shall not attempt here a thorough treatment of the research relevant to the processes I will describe. Instead, I shall try to put each set of concepts into a language which not only makes sense to me but which communicates well to the layman.

In the consultant role I have often found it necessary to translate difficult psychological ideas into simple formulations. In that process one sometimes has to sacrifice rigor, but as long as one knows what the underlying theory and research findings are, it is worth while to translate concepts into something the client can understand and deal with. One of the reasons why the layman should be cautious in using the kind of consultation process I am describing is that he is less likely than the expert to be aware of the degree to which the simple formulations of interpersonal and group process distort the underlying theory and research findings, and therefore less able to compensate for whatever distortion is introduced in the service of better communication.

Since the focus is first to be on the *diagnosis* of process events, I will draw on observations made during consultation work with various clients. (How I came to be in the group, how I made contact and set goals with the client, and how I chose an intervention strategy will be treated in detail in Part 2 of this book.) This choice of sequence is based on the assumption that it is important to understand initially how the process consultant views his client system and what things he looks for. Having gained some insight into organizational processes, the layman can then understand more easily how the process consultant defines his role and works with his client.

Most of the illustrations which will be given come from my work *with groups of various sorts.* This fact should not be taken to imply that working on interpersonal events in groups is the same thing as OD. Rather, the work of the process consultant with groups in the organization can be thought of as one key step in an OD program. Often it is the *first* step, in that it brings to managers an awareness of process, which in turn makes it possible for them to think in more developmental terms. Equally often it is a necessary step in the middle of an OD program in building strength and linking together individuals from different functions.

How is a team built or strengthened? How are intergroup relations improved? How does the OD specialist implement his strategies? Most often the answer to all of these questions is "by a variety of P-C efforts." In explicating P-C in detail, therefore, I am trying to expose some of the day-to-day events that may occur as part of an OD effort.

To recap, the key to Process Consultation is the combination of skill in (1) establishing a helping relationship; (2) knowing what kinds of processes to look for in organizations; and (3) intervening in such a way that organizational processes are improved.

3
COMMUNICATION PROCESSES

One of the most important processes in organizations, and one of the easiest to observe, is how the members communicate with each other, particularly in face-to-face situations. Many formulations of communication depict it as a simple problem of transfer of information from one person to another. But, as all of us know, the process is anything but simple, and the information transferred is often highly variable and highly complex. We communicate facts, feelings, perceptions, innuendos, and various other things all in the same "simple" message. We communicate not only through the spoken and written word but through gesture, physical posture, tone of voice, timing of when we speak, what we do not say, and so on. The present chapter will attempt to start with simple observables about communication and then will move into "deeper," less observable communication processes.

WHO COMMUNICATES? HOW OFTEN? FOR HOW LONG?

The easiest analysis of communication is to focus only on the *relative frequency* and *duration* of communication acts. Thus, if the observer wishes to study the communication behavior of a group or committee, he can list the names of all the members and put a check mark next to a name each time that person says something. He can measure duration by putting down a checkmark every few seconds as long as the speaker continues.

After some period of time the chart can be summarized to show who has talked, how often, and how much of the total available time he has used. One can also determine who used short communications and who spoke for long periods. If one wanted to analyze written communications, an analogous chart could be set up to determine who sends, how often he sends, and how long the message.

I have deliberately ignored things like the content of the message, in order to illustrate that even very simple things can be observed and learned from. For example, in my experience both in training groups and in meetings, a frequent occurrence is that one or more "quiet" members are accused by the more vocal ones of not contributing their thoughts to the discussion. In many instances I have heard the "quiet" members deny this accusation, saying that they had been talking but that apparently no one had been listening to them. To help the group focus on this kind of issue, it can be extremely valuable to have a record of how many times each person actually spoke relative to other persons. In most instances of this sort, I have found that the "silent" member is quite right; he had spoken several times but others had stereotyped him as silent and hence not heard what he had to say. Once the facts are recognized, it is possible to move on to the more important issue of *why* it is that some members are listened to more than others.

It should be noted that the process consultant helps the group by gathering data, but when and how he uses these data will depend very much on his judgment of how ready the group is to look at its own process. The key assumption *always* is that the group or the individual manager who is the client must collaborate in formulating the diagnosis. Therefore nothing is gained by a premature feedback of data which will be either ignored or resisted.

Even though the consultant may have made extensive analysis of the group's communication patterns, he may withhold all of the data until such time as he senses that the group is ready. Furthermore, sensing when the group is ready calls for a complex judgment based on other observations which I will describe below. The consultant cannot treat a simple request as equivalent to being ready. All too often I have had a group ask me for my observations of the group's process, only to find once I began to share these observations, that the group had trapped me into a position where I could be neutralized by being shown by some members how "wrong" my observations were.

WHO COMMUNICATES TO WHOM?

The next level of complexity of observation would be to determine who talks or writes to whom. Such observation is not difficult with written communications if they are addressed, but it can be quite tricky in a group situation since people often are not very explicit about whom they are directing themselves to. The observer may have to watch the speaker's eyes to see whom he is looking at when he is talking, or he may observe bodily posture for similar cues. These observations, like the previous set, could be recorded in a matrix where all the members are listed on both the horizontal and vertical axis and a check mark is made in the appropriate cell of the matrix. Alternatively, the method could extend the previous one by simply listing for each communication who the speaker and who the recipients were.

This level of communication analysis can reveal a number of processes. For example, if one tracks who speaks to whom fairly carefully, one quickly discovers that some members talk to the whole group, some talk to the ceiling or floor, and some members have favorite audiences. Having identified, for example, the fact that Joe tends mostly to direct his comments at Pete, the question arises as to why this occurs, leading to a next level of observation of their behavior. At this next level it may turn out that Joe talks mostly to Pete because the latter tends to agree with everything the former says. A kind of a subgroup or coalition exists within the larger group, which may have a variety of implications for the functioning of the total group.

Alternatively, I have found that sometimes people talk to those others from whom they expect the most opposition or resistance. Thus, Joe may have learned that Pete is the member most likely to "shoot him down." He talks first to Pete to see whether he can expect to get his point past what he sees to be his toughest hurdle.

The above illustration highlights the fact that any given set of observations which the consultant makes do not mean anything very significant in and of themselves. Rather, the observations of regularities and key events in group communication serve as a guide or a set of cues for progressively more meaningful questions which then determine new areas of observation. For example, if the manager of the group exhibits a bias in terms of whom he tends to talk to in his meetings, this fact by itself means relatively little. But if the consultant observes how the members who are and are not talked to by the boss *react* to this behavior, he can formulate some important hypotheses about the functioning of the group.

WHO TALKS AFTER WHOM? WHO INTERRUPTS WHOM?

Closely related to the issue of who talks to whom is the matter of who triggers whom and in what ways. I have noted in observing groups that there are clear patterns of triggering. Whenever Joe speaks the odds are pretty good that Pete will be the next to speak even if the remarks were not initially directed at him. Again, this may reflect either support or a desire to undo the point which Joe has made. As every observant group member has noted many times, such undoing can take the most elaborately polite forms, yet it remains as a "Yes, *but* . . . ." reaction nevertheless. As one group member once put it, in his company examples of such encouragement or undoing are labeled "Attaboys" and "Yeabuts," and the norm is that it takes at least three attaboys to undo the damaging effect of one yeabut in the group discussion.

Sometimes this level of analysis seems trivial, superficial, and contrived. If the observer's analysis stopped at this level, it would indeed be insufficient. What we need to underline again is that the overt surface behavior provides the clues as to what is going on between the people beneath the surface. Such clues not only help the process consultant understand what is going on, but are a visible manifestation to the members themselves. If the process consultant's role is to set up a situation of shared diagnosis, he must concentrate on observables which are as readily seen by the clients as by him. One of the great problems of psychologically sophisticated consultants who forget their mission as defined here is that they correctly interpret to the group what is happening but the interpretation is so far detached from observable behavior that the group members reject both it and the consultant.

Let us now turn to the other kind of behavior mentioned in the heading: who interrupts whom. The importance of observing this type of communication behavior derives from the fact that it gives us clues as to how members perceive their own status or power in the group relative to the status or power of other members. It is a matter of common observation, and has been documented in careful studies of deference, that the person of higher rank, status, or power feels free to interrupt someone of lower rank. We generally let the boss finish his sentences more often than he lets us finish ours. In those instances where this trend seems not to hold, one often finds that the members feel themselves to be of equal status even though objectively their rank may be different. Even then they might be more careful in public than in private situations.

Assuming a working team of "equals," what does it mean if the marketing man often interrupts the production man, but the reverse seldom occurs? The process consultant would ask himself whether there was in fact a status difference, or, if not, whether the marketing man simply felt himself to be more important than the production man. In the latter case, a fairly common kind of problem arises from the fact that the production man begins to feel a loss of influence, to which he may react by starting to fight the marketing man rather than continuing to work cooperatively with him.

Without insight on the part of either as to how they are signaling their feeling in overt communication acts, it is difficult for them to improve their working relationship. Only if the consultant can create a situation where they discover for themselves how their self-perceptions, perceptions of each other, and subjective judgments about their own influence relative to others, come out in overt behavior, can they improve the relationship.

In general, it has been my observation that interrupting others is one of the more common and more destructive kinds of communication behavior. Most people have relatively little awareness of how often and how crudely they cut in on others, convinced that what they have to say is more important than what they believe the previous speaker would have continued to say. When this process is itself interrupted by a consultant intervention, it often turns out that the person who first interrupted did not in fact really understand what the previous speaker was trying to say. In his eagerness he was formulating his own thoughts rather than listening to what was said before him.

One of the unfortunate consequences of frequent interruption is that the group is likely to interpret this as a sign of lack of organization. The suggestion is usually made that the way to control interruptions and avoid having too many people talking at once is to give the chairman more power to cut people off, call on people, and generally establish order. This solution substitutes external discipline for internal control. It misdiagnoses the problem as one of organization rather than recognizing it as a problem of lack of concern of the members for each other, resulting in insufficient listening. If the problem is one of listening, then the formal-chairmanship solution will not deal with the problem. Members will still not listen, but will instead be busy formulating what they will say when called upon.

COMMUNICATION STYLE

Communication style is intended to refer to a whole range of things such as whether the person is assertive, questioning, pedantic, or humorous;

whether his tone of voice is loud, soft, grating, or melodious; whether he accompanies his words with gestures, and so on. Insofar as the process consultant is interested in member relations, he is less concerned about style as an indicator of underlying personality, and more concerned about the possible effects of a given communication style on the others with whom the person is communicating.

For example, I may notice that a person talks very loudly and assertively, causing others gradually to "tune him out," yet he seems to be quite unaware that this is happening. He may even become aware of his declining influence in the group, and yet remain unaware of what has caused this decline. He does not hear himself as loud and assertive. The other members of the group who are no longer paying attention to him are also in a trap. They may not be paying attention because of the communication style used by the speaker and because they erroneously feel that it is the content of what he is saying which is failing to hold their interest. Communication in this situation cannot improve until both parties to the problem gain some insight into what they are doing and why they are doing it (e.g., what cues they are sending and are reacting to).

GESTURAL COMMUNICATION (KINESICS)

As anthropologists and linguists have known for some time, bodily posture, gestures, facial expressions, and other nonverbal behavior can and do become patterned according to the culture in which the person grew up. To the extent that they are patterned and have symbolic meanings, they can be understood just as clearly as verbal or written communication. Certain gestures, for example, reflect ethnic background. It has been shown by careful analysis of films of people in spontaneous interaction that some groups (e.g., first-generation Jewish immigrants) tend to accompany assertive words with forward reaching one-handed gestures, often described as "buttonholing." First-generation Italians, in contrast, tend to use both hands in gesturing and to rotate them outwards rather than pointing toward the listener.

Hall, in his excellent book *The Silent Language*, describes a whole range of culturally determined nonverbal cues which must be understood if the listener is to make correct interpretations of the speaker. For example, in every culture there is a kind of "ideal sphere" around a person. This "sphere" is the territory or space around a person which may not be violated unless you are on intimate terms with him, have some legitimate reason, or are deliberately and aggressively violating it.

Examples of violation would be standing too close, touching, etc. In countries where this "normal" distance is less than in America, the American is likely to feel uncomfortable because people are always standing too close in conversation or getting him into corners.

Systematic observation of postural and gestural behavior have been made by Birdwhistell (1961), using methods of analysis first developed in the field of linguistics. This field of analysis he calls *kinesics*. He has identified, for example, some of the nonverbal behavior which is associated with courtship patterns and which is properly labeled as "preening." It can be observed that a young man, when he suddenly finds himself in the company of an attractive girl, will straighten his tie, pull up his socks, run his fingers through his hair, adopt a slightly more erect posture, and have a higher muscle tonus. If the girl similarly notices the young man and responds to him she will also show higher muscle tonus, may flush slightly, stroke her hair, check her makeup, straighten her stockings, and sketchily rearrange her clothing (Scheflen, 1965). Further postural and nonverbal cues are also associated with what Scheflen identified as stages of "positioning for courtship" and "actions of invitation." Since such cues are culturally learned, their meaning is clear to members of the same culture.

Though methods of analysis of such complex gestures are still in their infancy, it is not too difficult to imagine that they could be successfully used in identifying cues which accompany aggressiveness, excessive deference, boredom, and various other feelings which are of great importance in group situations. In fact, I suspect that most experienced managers already rely on many such clues but do so unsystematically and without complete awareness of what it is on which they are relying.

LEVELS OF COMMUNICATION

So far I have discussed more or less manifest and easily observable communication events. In order to make some sense of these events and to understand more fully how members of any encounter react to each other, it is important to analyze less easily observable events. As background for this discussion some psychological theory about the nature of communication is also relevant.

As most of us know from observation of our own behavior, not only do we tend to react to the manifest content of what another person says to us, but we interpret what he says and use various subtle clues to get at the real meaning of the message. Often the same message carries more than one meaning, both a manifest and a latent meaning. Occasionally these meanings tend to contradict each other. Simple examples would be the person who issues an invitation with the statement "Come over to our house anytime," but leaves it sufficiently ambiguous through his tone of voice to make you realize that he does not really want you to come but is merely being polite. In work teams it is not unusual for a person to argue against a proposal because he feels he has to be consistent with a previous position or because he feels he must defend a group whom he represents, but to argue in such a way as to let it be known that he is privately prepared to be convinced and will go along eventually. Often we say one thing in order to "save face" but manage to communicate something else.

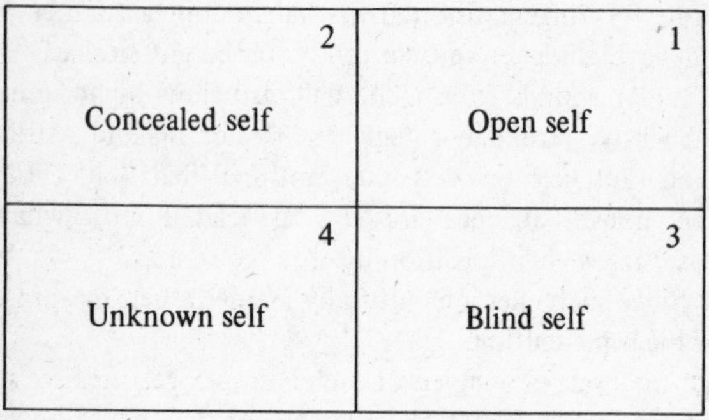

2 Concealed self	1 Open self
4 Unknown self	3 Blind self

Fig. 3.1 The parts of a person.*

Double messages of this kind do not pose unusual difficulties because the sender is aware of them and can clarify misunderstandings. Greater difficulty arises from double messages which reflect parts of the person of which he is unaware. To illustrate what is meant it is useful to think of the person as having several parts as depicted in Fig. 3.1. Quadrant 1 in the figure represents those areas of the person of which he himself is aware and which he is willing to share with others: the "open self." Quadrant 2 represents those parts of himself of which he is aware, but which he is consciously and deliberately trying to conceal from others. Typical examples which come up if one asks a group to reveal anonymously some of the things they conceal from others are areas of insecurity which the person is ashamed to admit, feelings and impulses which he considers to be antisocial or inconsistent with his self-image, memories of events where he failed or showed up particularly badly against his own standards, and,

*   J. Luft, "The Johari Window," *Hum. Rel. Tr. News* 5, 1961, pp. 6-7.

most importantly, feelings and reactions to other people which he feels would be impolite or hurtful to reveal.

For example, Joe might think that the boss made a terrible presentation at the key meeting, leading to loss of the sale, but equally might feel he must withhold this reaction and compliment the boss "in order not to hurt his feelings or make him mad." As we will see later, one of the key insights resulting from P-C is understanding of how much valuable loss of communication results from conscious concealment of reactions to interpersonal events.

Quadrant 3 in the figure is the key one for this discussion. The "blind area" of the self refers to those things which we unconsciously conceal from ourselves yet which are part of us and which are communicated to others. "I am *not* angry" says the boss in loud tones, purple-faced, as he slams his fist on the table. "These meetings are quite relaxing for me" says the executive as his hand trembles, his voice cracks, and he either has a third martini or tries unobtrusively to slip a tranquilizer into his mouth. "I do not care about the opinions of others," says the manager, but then he gets very upset if others do not notice him or his work.

All of us have, in the process of growing up, been rewarded for being certain kinds of people and punished for being other kinds. The young boy learns that it is all right to have aggressive feelings but that it is not all right to feel fear or tenderness when with other boys. So he begins to reject feelings of tenderness as being not part of himself. He suppresses them or refuses to recognize them as his own when they occur. Yet they may be quite visible to other people. How often have we said of a very gruff, tough man that he is really very tender. What we are saying is that we see tender behavior but that the person himself cannot see his own tender side and must continue to deny it by a gruff exterior. I have seen executives who became aggressive in direct proportion to the amount of tenderness they felt for the men around them; and I have seen women who became studiously considerate and tender in direct proportion to the amount of aggression they were feeling but unwilling to admit to themselves.

Each of us thus has feelings and traits which we feel are not part of us, and we are blind to the fact that we do communicate many such feelings to others. We may also be blind to the fact that some of the feelings which we try to conceal do "leak out."

Quadrant 4 consists of those parts of the person of which neither he nor others are aware. Examples would be truly unconscious and deeply repressed feelings and impulses, hidden talents or skills, potentialities, and so on. For our purposes this area is irrelevant.

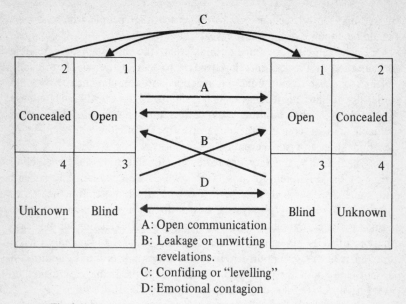

A: Open communication
B: Leakage or unwitting
   revelations.
C: Confiding or "levelling"
D: Emotional contagion

Fig. 3.2 Types of messages in a two-person communication situation.

Let us now consider two people in interaction with each other (Fig. 3.2) and analyze the implications of the different kinds of messages and different levels of communication which occur. Most communication occurs between the two open selves of the persons (Arrow A), and most popularized analyses of the communication process confine themselves to this level.

A second level of communication is the signals or meanings which we pick up from a person's blind self and which he is unaware of sending (Arrows B).

A third level of communication occurs when we deliberately reveal something which we ordinarily tend to conceal (Arrow C). Ordinarily we think of this as "confiding" in someone or "leveling" if we are sharing reactions or feelings generated by immediate events.

Finally, there is a less common but no less important level of communication represented by Arrow D which might best be labeled "emotional contagion." One person influences the feelings of another without either one's being consciously aware of the origin of the feeling. Sometimes the feeling which is aroused in the recipient mirrors that of the sender, as when tension which may be denied by the sender nevertheless makes the receiver tense as well. In other cases the feeling is different, as when a denied but displayed feeling in one person causes tension in the other because he does not know whether he should respond to the manifest level of communication (the denial of feeling) or to the latent level (the actually displayed feeling).

The implications of this analysis for the process consultant are that he must be aware of these subtleties and complications in levels of communication in order to understand fully the flow of interpersonal events. I have observed a group situation where the senior executive and chairman of the group became very angry at several members and punished them openly for failing to follow through on a project. Yet surprisingly, he did not arouse any defensiveness or tension on their part. The explanation was that they had learned over a long period of time that he was really frustrated over not being more involved in the project himself and was really communicating, without being aware of it, that he was feeling sorry for himself. His group reacted more to this second message and worked hard to involve him in the project. When they succeeded, his anger subsided. What this executive was unconsciously denying was his need to be involved and needed (a very tender feeling), yet these feelings were clearly perceived by his subordinates and they had no difficulty responding to them.

Once one recognizes several levels of communication, one can open up communication channels which ordinarily are not used. Once the participants in an interpersonal situation obtain some insight into their own communication behavior, it is possible for them to examine rationally the pros and cons of opening more of the Arrow C or "confiding" kind of channel. Specifically, they can examine whether or not effectiveness of the group would be increased if more members shared their private feelings, particularly feelings pertaining to other members and to the work situation.

A very common situation which the consultant faces is that members of a work group or team will reveal feelings such as frustration, anger, futility, tenderness, or concern privately to him, but it never occurs to them to share these feelings with the people who elicit them. The reasons for such withholding are multiple:—Our culture says it is not polite; it may seem hurtful to the other person; there is the danger of angering the other person leading to retaliation on his part; it may make the relationship too intimate; or it is something which simply does not occur to the person to do.

One powerful effect of sensitivity training is to open up these kinds of communications, but the process consultant is often working with a group that has had no experience with T-groups and is unwilling to experiment with them. In this instance the consultant can still stimulate more open communications by interventions which show the group the price of *not* communicating at this level. The approach would be to start with rather safe topics and areas. A member is against a proposal but instead of sharing his feeling he starts various political maneuvers to ensure that the proposal will not go through, or, worse, lets it go through and then resists implementing it. If the consultant can get the group to spend some time analyzing its own process, he can raise the question of how members originally felt about the proposal, and thus stimulate in a safer environment some opening up of earlier feelings. If this exercise proves illuminating and productive to the group, they are likely to be a bit more open in the next work session, though the consultant has to expect this kind of learning to be very slow and erratic.

Exploration of the B type of communication is most relevant if the group is having serious communication problems. The consultant can then raise the question of whether members are confusing each other by sending more than one message at once, creating for the recipient the problem of which one to react to. It should be noted that if the group agrees to discuss this issue at all, the members must reveal some of their own reactions. In other words, if I tell someone that he is sending a B-type message, thus reducing one of his blind spots, I am at the same time revealing something of my reactions which I ordinarily hide, thus reducing the size of my own concealed areas. Discussions of either B- or C-type messages tend thus to stimulate each other. The desired result would be a situation in which all members could enlarge their own open areas in their dealings with each other, thereby reducing distortions, miscommunications, and ambiguities.

FILTERING

The final, and perhaps most difficult, complexity to consider in the communication process is that both the sender and the receiver use a number of filters in selecting what they will send and what they will receive. I am not implying conscious censorship, though this occurs also. Rather, I am implying that all of us select what we say, how we say it, and when we say it in terms of a complex set of decision rules which we have learned over a lifetime and which reflect a number of specific factors:

a) *Self-image*. Both the sender and the receiver have an image or concept of themselves and feelings of self-worth or self-esteem. What their self-concept is at any given time and what value they attach to themselves in a given situation will, in part, determine their communication. For example, if I think of myself as an expert in an area and have great confidence in myself (attach great worth to myself) in a given situation, I am more likely to communicate in the first place, more likely to choose an assertive, telling style of communication rather than a diffident one, and less likely to listen to others on that same topic. After all, I am the expert.

b) *Image of the Other Person or Persons.* Both the sender and the receiver have an image or concept of the others in the situation and attach certain values to these others as people. These images of the "other" will also, in part, determine communication. For example, if I see the others in the situation as being less expert and of lower status in the situation than I am, I am likely to talk down to them, to interrupt them when I think they are off target, to listen less for their original points of view and more for whether they are understanding me and/or agreeing with me. If I feel less expert or of lower status I will say less, listen harder, and try to figure out how to gain status in the situation (this, incidentally, may inhibit good listening also, diverting attention from the task to the relationship issue).

c) *Definition of the Situation.* Both the sender and the receiver have a certain picture of the situation they are jointly operating in. Is it a meeting to solve a specific problem? Is it an informal bull session? Are we here to give the boss a chance to tell us his ideas, and so on? Often this process of "defining the situation" is not verbalized until someone raises the question "What are we here for?" or "What is our task?"

The definition of the situation goes beyond specifying the goals or task to be achieved; it is the complete set of perceptions pertaining to one's own and others' roles in the situation, its duration, its boundaries, and the norms which will govern it (e.g., is it a formal or informal situation?). Obviously, what we say and how we say it will be largely governed by how we define the situation.

d) *Motives, Feelings, Intentions, Attitudes.* Another set of filters on the communication process both for sender and listener are the various needs and motives they bring to the situation, their intentions, and their attitudes toward others. If my needs are to sell a proposal or to influence others, I will communicate differently than if I am curious about something and need to get information. If I am trying to influence I will listen differently and for different things in what others say than if I am gathering information. For example, if I am trying to influence, I will listen harder for agreement or disagreement than for new ideas.

e) *Expectations.* The final category of psychological factors which create filters is our expectations of ourselves and of others in the situation, based either on actual experience or on preconceptions and stereotypes. If I expect my audience to be slow to understand, I will use simpler words; if I expect them to be receptive, I will talk in a more relaxed way; if I expect them to be critical, I will frame my points carefully and precisely. From the point of view of the listener, if he expects the speaker to be very smart, he may read in more meaning than there is in the message; if he expects him to be inarticulate or unintelligent, he may fail to hear the good points. If he expects disagreement he may read hostility into what the speaker says; and if he expects support he may fail to hear disagreement.

Given all the various filters described, it is not surprising that the communication process between people is fraught with so much difficulty. The process consultant is not immune to the psychological factors described. He will have his own set of filters based upon his needs, expectations, images, intentions, and so on. Because he is a trained observer he may spot the effects of filters sooner than other members, but he certainly cannot see the truth in any absolute sense any better than any other member can. It is partly for this reason that he must help the group to make a diagnosis rather than simply providing his own diagnosis as if it were the absolute truth. It is only out of the joint efforts of all the members that a diagnosis of communications difficulties can be made which is likely to be near enough to the truth to warrant remedial action.

The Circular Process and Self-fulfilling Prophecies

The various factors described above under the category of filtering make it possible for communications to break down in a particularly dangerous manner. If expectations are strong on the part of both the sender and the receiver, it is possible for each to interpret the cues from the other in such a way that both confirm their stereotypes and thus "lock" each other into roles from which it is difficult to escape. Let us take two examples.

Person A, on the basis of previous experience, has a very positive self-image, is confident, needs to influence others, and expects to be able to do so. His communications are assertive, confident, and clear. His listeners respond to this clarity and assertiveness by paying attention to what he has to say, thus confirming A's image of himself as an influential person. He gains confidence from being listened to and assumes an increasingly strong role in the group.

Person B, on the basis of his previous experience, is not sure of himself, feels a lack of confidence in the presence of several others, is not sure he can influence people even though he would like to, and expects that he will have difficulty establishing himself in the group. His communications will, as a result, be hesitant, low key, and diffident, though they may be just as clear as A's. His listeners may well respond to the diffidence and hesitancy by assuming that B does not have much to offer and may cease to pay attention to him, thus confirming his own initial impression of himself as having little to contribute. B loses confidence, communicates less and less, further confirming for the others his lack of potential contribution, and gradually assumes the role of a noncontributor.

In both cases the final outcome is the result of initial expectations which produce a certain communication style, which in turn lead to confirmation of the initial expectations. The danger is that the initial expectations may have little to do with the actual potential contribution of A and B to the group product; yet A will be a high contributor and B will be a low contributor. Only by becoming sensitive to this kind of self-fulfilling prophecy can the group protect itself from getting a mix of contributions which are unrelated to actual ability.

A key role for the process consultant is to ask himself, when he observes different rates of participation and contribution to the group, whether this accurately reflects ability to contribute or is the result of circular processes of the sort described. If the consultant finds evidence for the latter, he must help the group reassess its own operations, reexamine its stereotypes of who can contribute what, and build norms which permit the low-confidence contributor to gain confidence by being listened to.

SUMMARY

In the previous sections I have examined various facets of the communication process. Starting with relatively overt processes like who talks, who talks to whom, who interrupts whom, and what style of communication is used, I then reviewed more subtle communication issues like the meaning implicit in nonverbal communication, the role of different levels of communication stemming from our blind spots and tendencies to conceal certain things about ourselves, and the problems stemming from our tendencies to filter in the role of both sender and receiver.

This set of issues by no means exhausts all aspects of communication which could be reviewed. For example, we did not cover problems of semantics; nor did we get into all the issues of how to say and show things in such a way as to be more persuasive—the kinds of things one might find in courses on "good" communications. Topics covered reflect those aspects of communication which tend to be especially important in work teams, staff meetings, bull sessions, committees, T-groups, and other settings where member relations have to be "good" in order for work output to be high. The process consultant must help the group to perceive the connection between the subtle communication process described and the kind of factual exchange which leads to effective working relations and high output.

4
FUNCTIONAL ROLES OF GROUP MEMBERS

One of the most salient observations in groups or interpersonal encounters is that different members and leaders do different things; or, to put it another way, their behavior serves different functions. There have been many attempts to categorize and describe the various functions or roles which group members perform in their interaction with each other. The system I will describe has not been used as extensively in laboratory research as some others, but has proved more useful in teaching an observer what is going on in a group.[1]

The underlying theoretical premise is that when two or more people come together to form a work- or task-oriented group, there will first be a period of essentially self-oriented behavior reflecting various concerns which any new member of a group could be expected to experience. As the self-oriented behavior declines, members begin to pay more attention to each other and to the task at hand. The kinds of behavior which help the group to build and maintain itself then occur concurrently with behaviors designed to accomplish the work of the group. I would like to describe the steps in a chronological sequence because they occur more or less in sequence, though each phase may overlap the others.

1   The categories used are based on Benne, K., and Sheats, P., "Functional roles of group members." *J. Soc. Iss.,* **2,** 1948, pp. 42-47.

PHASE 1: PROBLEMS IN ENTERING A NEW GROUP; SELF-ORIENTED BEHAVIOR

The problems which a person faces when he enters a new group stem from certain underlying emotional issues which must be resolved before he can feel comfortable in the new situation. Four such issues can be readily identified (see Fig. 4.1).

a) *Identity.* First and foremost is the problem of choosing a role or identity which will be acceptable to the person himself and viable in the group. In other words, each new member, whether he is aware of it or not, must find an answer to the question "Who and what am I to be in this group?"

This issue exists in the first place because all of us have a large repertory of possible roles and behavioral styles to bring into play in any given situation. Should I be the dominant aggressive leader, a behavior pattern which may have worked for me in some situations; or should I be the humorous tension reliever, which may have worked for me in other situations; or should I be the quiet listener, which has worked in still other situations? In varying degrees we are different people in the different life situations we operate in. Therefore we always have some degree of choice in new situations.

In *formal* committees or work groups, this kind of issue is often partially resolved through the initial mandate. A person is told to join a task force to represent the personnel point of view, or a strong chairman tells members what kinds of role he wants them to play. Such resolutions are at best only partial, however, in that there is still great latitude for the person to develop a style which will satisfy him and be acceptable to the others in the group. As Fig. 4.1 indicates, as long as the emotional issue is there, whether the person recognizes it consciously or not, it operates as a source of tension, leads the person to be primarily preoccupied with himself, and consequently leads to less listening and concern for others or the group task.

b) *Control, Power, Influence.* A second issue which a new member faces and which must be resolved in any new group is the distribution of power and influence. It can be safely assumed that every member will have *some* need to control and influence others, but the amount of this need and its form of expression will vary from person to person. One member may wish to influence the actual task solution, another may wish to influence the methods or procedures used by the group, a third may wish to achieve an overall position of prominence in the group, and so on.

The dilemma for all members early in the group's history is that they do not know each other's needs or styles, and hence cannot easily determine who will be able to influence whom and what. Consequently the consultant will frequently observe a great deal of fencing, testing each other out, and experimenting with different forms of influence in early meetings. The consultant must be careful not to misunderstand this behavior. On the surface it seems like a definite flight from whatever task the group is facing. Underneath it represents an important sorting out, getting acquainted, and coming to terms with each other which the members need to do in order to relax their self-concerns and focus on the task.

If a chairman insists on a tight formal schedule which prevents some of this kind of getting acquainted and testing out, he runs the risk of either producing superficial solutions because members are not ready to really work on the task, or of forcing them to do their fencing in the context of the task work, thereby slowing down the progress and undermining the potential quality of the solution. In this kind of situation, the consultant must help the chairman to understand what functions the initial sorting-out behavior performs for the members, to understand the need for group building time, and to understand that good communications cannot develop until members' self-preoccupations have been reduced.

c) *Individual Needs and Group Goals.* A third issue which faces every group member is his concern that the group goals which are initially set or which will emerge from discussion may not include his personal goals and needs. Preoccupation with this issue typically leads the person to wait and see how the group develops, not to invest himself too heavily in it until he sees whether things will go his way or not. The problem for the group as a whole is that if a substantial number of people take the wait-and-see attitude, it is difficult to get any group action started. In this situation the group typically turns to any available authority to set the agenda, formulate goals, or suggest a task. If the chairman responds to the pressure and sets the goals, he is partially solving the problem, but he still cannot ensure that the goals he sets will involve all the members sufficiently to get them committed to the task.

A sounder procedure would be to face the paradox directly: *until member needs are to some degree exposed and shared, it is not possible to set up valid group goals.* Consequently, enough meeting time should be allocated to permit members to explore what they really want to get out of the group. The role of the process consultant in this situation is usually to slow down the group and to reassure members that the early struggles to communicate with each other are a necessary and important part of group growth.

d) *Acceptance and Intimacy.* These two issues are lumped together because they deal with the same underlying problem: Will I be liked and accepted by the others in the group, and how close or intimate will we have to be to achieve a comfortable level of mutual respect and acceptance? For every set of people and every situation norms must be developed by the group which help to resolve these issues. There is no optimal or absolute level of acceptance and intimacy for all groups at all times. It depends on the members, on the group task, on the length of time available to the group, and a host of other factors. But the issue is always there as a source of tension until working norms have been established.

Initially the issue will appear in terms of forms of address and patterns of politeness. As the group develops, the issue will center around formality or informality of group procedures. At a still later stage the issue will center on whether group discussion must stick to the formal task or whether more personal exchanges are permissible and desirable. In training groups the issue usually revolves around the amount of self-disclosure which is necessary and desirable to optimize the learning process.

The group can attempt to legislate solutions by the adoption of Roberts' Rules of Order or similar devices, but such procedures are more likely to sweep the issue under the rug than really to resolve it. The role of the process consultant can be to help the group to recognize that the issue is a legitimate one to be worked on.

Types of Coping Responses to Emotional Issues

As has been indicated above, each of the underlying problems in gaining membership leads to tension, frustration, and self-preoccupation. What does the person typically do in coping with the underlying problems and the resulting tensions? Three basic kinds of coping patterns can be observed:

1. basically tough aggressive coping,

2. basically tender, support-seeking coping, and

3. withdrawal behavior based on denial of any feelings. (See Figure 4.1.)

Problems	Resulting feelings	Coping responses (self-oriented)
1. *IDENTITY*		1. *"TOUGH" RESPONSES*
Who am I to be?	Frustration	Fighting, controlling resisting authority.
2. *CONTROL & INFLUENCE*		2. *"TENDER" RESPONSES*
Will I be able to control and influence others?	Tension	Supporting, helping forming alliances, dependency.
3. *NEEDS & GOALS*	Anxiety	3. *WITHDRAWAL OR DENIAL RESPONSES*
Will the group goals include my own needs?		Passivity, indifference, overuse of "logic and reason"
4. *ACCEPTANCE & INTIMACY*		
Will I be liked and accepted by the group? How close a group will we be?		

Fig. 4.1 Problems in entering a new group which cause self-oriented behavior.

The *tough, aggressive response* shows up in various kinds of fighting such as arguing, cutting down other members' points, ridiculing, deliberate ignoring of others, cutting and hostile humor, and the like. Though the behavior may be perfectly legitimate within the rules of group discussion under the guise of "debating the point" or "exploring our differences," the observer should be careful to note whether the underlying feelings expressed are really concern for a better task solution or are, in fact, ways of challenging and testing other members in the process of solving emotional issues such as have been identified above.

The aggressive response also is reflected in attempts to control other members through setting up procedures, calling on people, telling other members what they should be talking about, and the like. With respect to any authority figures in the group such as the chairman, this type of emotional behavior shows up as "counterdependency." Counter-dependency refers to feelings of wanting to resist authority. "Let's find out what the chairman wants us to do and then *not* do it, or let's do it our own way, not the way he wants us to do it."

In most formal groups such behavior is likely to be quite subtle because standards of politeness and formal power differences militate against open expressions of counterdependency. Yet it is not difficult for the process consultant to observe such behavior, to help the group to recognize the legitimacy of it, and to help differentiate emotional coping from genuine expression of differences on the task level.

The *tender, support-seeking response* is reflected in a variety of ways. Members look for someone with whom they seem to agree and try to form a supportive alliance or subgroup within the larger group. Members attempt to avoid conflict, give support, help each other, and generally try to suppress aggressive divisive feelings. With respect to authority, such behavior shows up as dependency: looking for someone to lean on, to give guidance, and to solve the problems which the members feel they have.

How does the process consultant differentiate this kind of behavior from constructive problem-solving behavior? First, he would note at what point in the group's or member's history the behavior is occurring. As I have indicated, the emotionally based self-oriented behavior occurs early in the history when members are trying to establish themselves in the group. The same kind of behavior later could simply mean genuine support in reference to the task.

A second criterion would be whether the consultant feels that the support is based on genuine mutual understanding or is a kind of blind response. The emotionally based behavior I am describing here is often indicated by members forming alliances without really showing evidence of understanding each other's points of view at all. It is hasty support seeking, an indiscriminate helping, and an inappropriate kind of dependency, the real meaning of which the consultant must help the group to understand.

The *withdrawing or denial response* is characterized by a suppression of tension and feeling, often resulting in a rather passive, indifferent, bland kind of response. It is as if the person were saying "You fellows go ahead and fight it out and get this group rolling while I watch; I do not really have any feelings about it so I'll get on board when things get properly organized." Another version of this emotional behavior is for the person to argue that feelings have no place in group discussion, should be legislated out of existence, and suppressed at all costs. When a fight breaks out, the person says "Gentlemen, we are all civilized, mature individuals; we can settle this logically and calmly. Let us not let our feelings get the better of us; let's stick to the facts."

If the person were being truly rational and logical, he would realize that the feelings in the situation are some of the facts which must be reckoned with. They can be suppressed and legislated off the agenda, but they cannot be made to disappear and they cannot be prevented from affecting each member's problem-solving behavior. If a group member has tensions and self-preoccupations, he will in fact not be listening to or concerned about other members, and hence will not contribute to effective problem-solving.

Each of us, as human beings, is capable of each of these basic types of response in our efforts to cope with the emotional issues of the group. Which style of response we tend to use will depend on our personalities, on our past histories in interpersonal situations, on the behavior of other members in the group, and on the formality and structure of the situation. For example, a formal, tightly controlled group is much more likely to produce withdrawal and denial responses which in the long run will produce a poorly motivated, alienated group. When such a group tries to solve a difficult problem there is no guarantee that members will be motivated enough to direct their energies to the problem, or able to communicate with each other well enough to build a genuine group solution. Permitting and exploring emotional expressions, on the other hand, will lead to initial discomfort but will, in the long run, produce a higher level of communication and a stronger, more effective group.

Resolution of Emotional Issues

I have described four kinds of emotional issues which face every person when he enters a new group situation—the problem of identity, the problem of influence and power, the problem of needs and goals, and the problem of acceptance and intimacy. Until the person finds a role for himself in the group and until the group develops norms pertaining to goals, influence, and intimacy, he will be tense and will respond in various emotional ways.

The price of such behavior for the group is that the members are preoccupied with their own feelings and hence less able to listen to each other and solve problems. Yet every group must go through some growing pains while members work on these issues and find their place. If the formal structure does not permit such growth, the group never becomes a real group capable of group effort. It remains a collection of individuals held together by a formal structure.

The process consultant can help the group to resolve emotional issues in a number of ways. First of all he must himself be aware of what is going on and not become anxious over the initial communication problems which members have. Secondly, he must help the group to realize that the early fighting, alliances, and withdrawal responses are efforts on the part of members to get to know each other, to test each other out, and to find their own place in the group. He can do this by giving the group perspective on itself through capsules of group theory of the sort I have given in the previous pages. He can indicate his belief that members are working on a legitimate group-building task, not just wasting time. Managers typically expect groups to be able to get right to work, and do not allow for a period of group building. If the group does not solve problems quickly they get angry and disillusioned with group effort. The process consultant must encourage such managers to be patient, to allocate enough time to group meetings to permit the group to grow, and to realize that their own anger and impatience is a reflection of the same emotional issues which the other members are facing.

Finally, the process consultant must be expert in giving helpful and useful feedback to members concerning their own behavior. Much of the coping is likely to be occurring without awareness on the part of the group members as to what is happening and why. If they are to gain some insight into this behavior and to become more expert in diagnosing it themselves, the consultant must try to help each member to understand his own coping behavior.

As members acquire this insight, as they begin to know how others are feeling and responding, and as members begin to realize that the group can include them and their potential contribution, there is a gradual relaxation and an increasing ability to pay attention to others. When this happens one can sense a change in the climate and mood of the group: There is less urgency, more listening, less running away from tasks to be performed, more willingness to cooperate as a total group, less formality and falling back on arbitrary rules, but more self-discipline and willingness to suppress personal agendas for the sake of the total group performance. The important thing to realize is that such a state can be achieved only if the group is permitted to work out its problem; it cannot be imposed or legislated.

PHASE 2: TASK AND GROUP-MAINTENANCE FUNCTIONS

So far I have discussed what happens in the early life of a group before it is really ready to solve problems effectively. In the following sections I will deal with various aspects of group problem-solving and the contributions which members make to it. Figure 4.2 shows a list of what have been called task functions and maintenance functions. These are behaviors

Task functions	Maintenance functions
Initiating	Harmonizing
Opinion Seeking	Compromising
Opinion Giving	Gatekeeping
Information Seeking	Encouraging
Information Giving	Diagnosing
Clarifying	Standard Setting
Elaborating	Standard Testing
Summarizing	
Consensus Testing	

Fig. 4.2 Task and maintenance functions in groups.*

which must occur to some degree in order for the group to progress effectively. From the point of view of the process consultant, the lists are important as a checking device to determine what kinds of functions are being performed adequately and what kinds of functions are either missing altogether or not adequately performed. The observer of process can also study the distribution of the functions to determine whether they are evenly distributed, whether some members consistently do one kind of thing, which functions the leader performs, and so on.

a) *Task Functions.* Let us look at some task functions first. In order for the group to make progress on a task there must be some *initiating*. Someone must state the goal or problem, make proposals as to how to work on it, set some time limits or targets, and the like. Often this function falls to the leader or to whoever called the group together in the first place, but it can be observed that as a group grows and gains confidence, initiating functions will increasingly come from a broader range of members.

In order for progress to be made there must be some *opinion seeking and giving,* and *information seeking and giving* on various issues related to the task. The kinds of information and opinions a group seeks in pursuing its tasks are often crucial for the quality of the solution. The observer should note carefully and help the group to observe for itself whether sufficient time was given to the information- and opinion-seeking functions. *Clarifying* and *elaborating* are critical functions in a group in order to test the adequacy of communication and in order to build on the

---

*   Benne and Sheats, *Op. cit.*

ideas of others towards more creative and complex ideas. If such activities do not occur, the group is not really using its unique strength.

Summarizing is an important function to ensure that ideas are not lost because of either the size of the group or the length of time of discussion. Effective summarizing will include a review of which points the group has already covered and what different ideas have been stated, so that as decision points are reached, the group is operating with full information. One common problem which I have observed in committees, task forces, and executive teams is that they tend to work sequentially and process one idea at a time, never gaining any perspective on the totality of their discussion. What is missing is the summarizing function. It can be fulfilled by having a recorder note ideas on a blackboard as the group proceeds so that it has its own visible summary before it at all times; or a person can, from time to time, simply review what he has heard and draw out tentative generalizations from it for the group to consider.

Finally, the group needs someone to periodically test whether it is nearing a decision or should continue to discuss. *Consensus testing* could involve simply asking the question "Are we ready to decide?" or could involve some summarizing: "It seems to me we have expressed these three alternatives and are leaning toward No. 2; am I right?" The success of this function in moving the group forward will depend largely on the sensitivity of the person in choosing the right time to test, though ill-timed tests are still useful in reminding the group that it has some more discussing to do.

Task functions such as these are so obviously relevant to effective group problem-solving that it is easy for the process consultant to get the group thinking of process in terms of them. One of the consultant's greatest problems is choosing what behavior to draw the group's attention to. The task functions provide one simple alternative which is not too likely to be resisted as irrelevant.

b) *Maintenance Functions.* In order for the group to survive and grow as an effective instrument of problem-solving, it is necessary for members to concern themselves with the maintenance of good relationships. Ideally such concerns would be expressed throughout the life cycle of the group, but, as we have already seen in the sections on the early phases of group life, members do become preoccupied with their own needs and thus may damage their relationships to others.

The problem for the group is how to rebuild damaged relationships and/or minimize initial tendencies for them to become damaged. By a damaged relationship I mean, for example, two members who are angry at each other because they have opposing views on a task issue, members who were outvoted or ignored and thus feel left out, members who feel misunderstood or sidetracked, and so on. In each case, the person is temporarily preoccupied with personal needs and feelings, and is therefore relatively less able to contribute to group effort. If no group maintenance occurs, the member is not brought back into harmony with the group, and is consequently lost as a resource to the group.

Some member activities can best be thought of as preventive maintenance. For example, the function of *gatekeeping* ensures that members who have a contribution to make to problem solution have an opportunity to make it. I have often sat in a group and observed one person repeatedly open his mouth and actually get one or two words out when a more aggressive person interrupts him, takes the floor away, and makes his own point. After two or three attempts, the person gives up, unless someone notices the problem and provides an opportunity for the person to get his point in. *Encouraging* may serve a similar function in helping a person make his point, partly to give the group the benefit of the content, but also to ensure that he and others will feel that the group climate is one of acceptance.

Harmonizing and *compromising* are deliberately placed on the maintenance function list rather than the task function list because they are useful in reducing destructive types of disagreement between individuals, but are definitely of limited usefulness in solving task problems. This is a crucial point because process consultants, in being concerned about group effectiveness, are likely to be seen as favoring harmony and smooth group functioning at all times. In fact, it may be quite necessary for the group to confront and work through tough disagreements to some genuine integrative solution which does not involve any compromising or harmonizing. The process consultant may often have to help the group to confront and work through a problem when it would rather back off and compromise. However, if communication has broken down and several members are arguing or taking positions because of self-oriented reasons such as maintaining their own status in the group, it may be necessary as a maintenance step to harmonize the conflict and help each member to take stock of his own behavior as a way of reestablishing good communication.

Diagnosing, standard setting and standard testing are most relevant as remedial measures when relationships have to some degree broken down. What the group then needs is some period of suspending task operations while it (1) looks at its process, checks out how people are feeling about the group, its norms, and its method of operating; and (2) permits airing of problems and conflicts which may have arisen. Most groups do not engage

Rating Group Effectiveness

A: Goals

Poor   1   2   3   4   5   6   7   8   9   10   Good
Confused; diverse;   Clear to all; shared
conflicting; indifferent;   by all; all care about
little interest.   the goals, feel
                                                           involved.

B: Participation

Poor   1   2   3   4   5   6   7   8   9   10   Good
Few dominate; some   All get in; all are
passive; some not   really listened to.
listened to; several
talk at once or
interrupt.

C: Feelings

Poor   1   2   3   4   5   6   7   8   9   10   Good
Unexpected; ignored   Freely expressed;
or criticized.   empathic responses.

D: Diagnosis of group problems

Poor   1   2   3   4   5   6   7   8   9   10   Good
Jump directly to   When problems arise
remedial proposals;   the situation is care-
treat symptoms   fully diagnosed before
rather than basic   action is proposed;
causes.   remedies attack basic
                                                           causes.

Fig. 4.3 Sample form for analyzing group effectiveness.

E: Leadership

Poor   1   2   3   4   5   6   7   8   9   10   Good

Poor	Good
Group needs for leadership not met; group depends too much on single person or on a few persons.	As needs for leadership arise various members meet them ("distributed leadership"); anyone feels free to volunteer as he sees a group need.

F: Decisions

Poor   1   2   3   4   5   6   7   8   9   10   Good

Poor	Good
Needed decisions don't get made; decision made by part of group; others uncommitted.	Consensus sought and tested; deviates appreciated and used to improve decision; decisions when made are fully supported.

G: Trust

Poor   1   2   3   4   5   6   7   8   9   10   Good

Poor	Good
Members distrust one another; are polite, careful, closed, guarded; they listen superficially but inwardly reject what others say; are afraid to criticize or to be criticized.	Members trust one another; they reveal to group what they would be reluctant to expose to others; they respect and use the responses they get; they can freely express negative reactions without fearing reprisal.

H: Creativity and growth

Poor   1   2   3   4   5   6   7   8   9   10   Good

Poor	Good
Members and group in a rut; operate routinely; persons stereotyped and rigid in their roles; no progress.	Group flexible, seeks new and better ways; individuals changing and growing; creative; individually supported.

in this kind of behavior unless a process consultant is present or one of the members takes a real process orientation. Yet such periods of reassessment and catharsis are absolutely necessary for most task groups if they are to remain effective.

How can the process consultant encourage the performance of these kinds of functions on a regular basis? One of the simplest techniques is to suggest that at every meeting (or on some periodic basis) the group allocate some small period of time such as 15 to 30 minutes to review its own meeting and to collect member feelings about how the meeting has gone. Such feelings can be collected in an open-ended way or with the help of diagnostic instruments such as that shown in Fig. 4.3. If an instrument is used, somewhat more time must be allocated to analysis. If the group is skeptical of the value of any diagnosis, it is better to start with short periods of open-ended discussion, keeping the instrument in reserve until the group learns the value of such discussions and is willing to allocate more time to them.

The role of the process consultant during diagnostic periods must be carefully managed. The great temptation is to rush in once the group has opened the door, and tell all the meaty observations which the consultant has made over the past several hours. This temptation is often heightened by the group's actually inviting the consultant to tell the group all of his observations. "How do you feel we did during the meeting?" "You've been sitting observing us for a couple of hours; what observations do you have?"

The process consultant must at this time remind himself what his basic mission is: to get the group to *share* in diagnosis and to help the group to *learn* to diagnose its own processes. If he succumbs and takes the lead in giving observations, there is great danger that the group will abdicate its own responsibility for diagnosis. Furthermore, if the consultant makes observations which some members disagree with, he quickly finds himself in a position of having been neutralized. Finally, if the consultant comes in with his own observations first, he is forgetting that his own filters are operating and that he may be reporting things which are relatively less important or which are a reflection of his own biases.

Given these pitfalls, it is important that the process consultant encourage the group not only to allocate time for diagnosis, but to take the lead itself in trying to articulate and understand its own processes. Once the group has identified an area where members themselves have observations to make, it is entirely appropriate for the consultant to add his own observations and to use the opportunity to deepen members' understanding by giving not only observations but some group theory. But the group must take the lead, and the consultant must work within the areas defined by the group as relevant. If the group urges the consultant to do this job *for them,* he must politely decline and urge the group in turn to try its own hand at diagnosis.

SUMMARY

Thus far we have been focusing on various aspects and functions of the individual's behavior in the group. We have examined the causes of self-oriented behavior and types of self-oriented behavior. We then examined various task functions relevant to getting a job done, and various maintenance functions relevant to keeping the group in good working order. Having dealt with these basics, let us proceed to an analysis of the processes involved in the actual work of the group: problem-solving and decision-making.

5
GROUP PROBLEM-SOLVING AND DECISION-MAKING

GROUP PROBLEM-SOLVING

Problem-solving as a process is much discussed and little understood. I propose to give the reader not *ultimately* valid models, but, as in past sections, *a* model which is amenable to observation and analysis. The steps or stages I will describe and analyze are applicable to *any* kind of problem-solving process whether it occurs in an individual manager, a two-person group, a large committee, or a total organization. My focus will remain, as in past sections, on the small group because it is in this size unit that the process consultant is more likely to be able to make his contribution.

The basic model as presented in Fig. 5.1 is an elaboration of a model developed by the late Richard Wallen. It distinguishes two basic cycles of activity—one which occurs *prior* to any decision or action, and one which occurs *after* a decision to act has been taken. The first cycle consists of:

1. problem formulation;

2. generating proposals for solution;

3. forecasting the consequences of solutions proposed or testing solutions and evaluating them conceptually before taking any action.

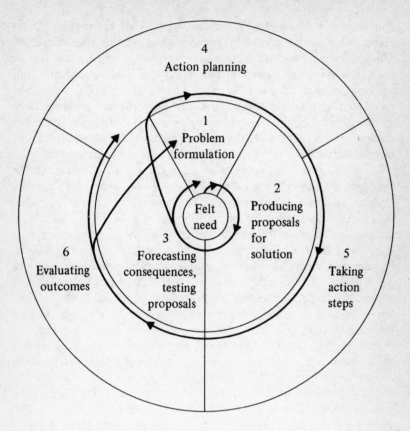

Fig. 5.1 A model of the stages of problem solving.

The second cycle involves:

4. action planning;

5. action steps; and

6. evaluation of outcomes, often leading back into the first cycle of problem definition.

Cycle 1

In my own experience in solving problems and watching others solve them, by all odds the most difficult step in this process is the first one—defining the problem. The difficulty arises in part because of a confusion between *symptoms* and the *problem.* A manager typically starts a problem-solving process when someone brings something to him or he discovers something which is not as it should be. Sales have fallen off, a schedule for delivery has not been met, an angry customer is on the phone, the production line has broken down, there is a fire in the shop, or whatever. But it should be noted that none of the things mentioned are really the problems to be worked on—rather they are the *symptoms to be removed.* Before the manager can begin to solve the problem he must identify or find it, and this is the crucial and often most difficult stage of the whole cycle.

Let us take the example of sales falling off, to illustrate the complexity. Manager X has called together his key subordinates and they sit down to discuss "the problem" of declining sales. If the manager is not sensitive to the issue raised above he may soon be in the midst of a discussion of whether the advertising budget should be raised or ten more men should be sent into the field. But has he as yet defined his problem? Has he even identified what the various *alternative problems* might be which could cause a reduction in sales? It could be anything from an erroneous sales forecast (which implies doing nothing out in the field but something in the marketing department) to a competitor's having entered the market suddenly. Without some *preliminary diagnosis* which, incidentally, may take time and effort, the manager won't know what is *really causing* the discrepancy between forecast and actual sales. He won't know what he should really be working on.

The process consultant can often play a key role at this stage because he is less likely to react to the time pressure which the manager is under, and, therefore is more likely to notice premature shortcuts in reasoning and misdiagnoses. His role is often to help the group to slow down and recognize that it may be acting hastily on an ill-defined problem, and that some initial time invested in identifying what is *really* the problem will pay off in less wasted time and effort later.

A special category of problems deserves particular mention in this regard—those involving interpersonal relations. A manager has a problem in motivating a subordinate, or coordinating with another department, or influencing his boss, or in integrating the effort of several people. Often these "problems" are felt as frustrations and tensions, with a minimum of clear understanding on the part of the manager of what is actually frustrating him or making him tense. In a sense he knows some things are not right, but he does not know what the problem really is.

In instances such as these, the process consultant can help the manager or the group to identify its problem by forcing them to produce

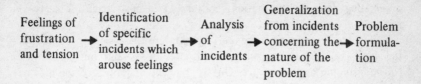

Fig. 5.2 Necessary steps in initially formulating the problem.

concrete incidents or examples of events which led to their feelings of frustration. By carefully going over these incidents in detail and trying to identify what was going on which actually triggered the frustration, it is often possible to define the real problem. The essential step is to examine the concrete incidents and to generalize the problem from these. This process can be thought of as a necessary stage of any problem formulation (Fig. 5.2). Once the problem has been adequately formulated, the group can move on to producing ideas or courses of action which might resolve the problem. At this stage the most likely pitfall is that proposals are evaluated one at a time; thus the group is never permitted to gain perspective on the problem by looking at a whole array of possible ideas for solution.

The process consultant can help here by pointing out the consequences of premature evaluation:

1. that there is insufficient opportunity for ideas to be judged in perspective because they cannot be compared to other ideas, and

2. that the evaluation tends to threaten not only a given idea but the person who proposed it. (Members whose ideas have been rejected early may feel less inclined to give ideas at a later stage.)

The technique of brainstorming is built on the rule that no *evaluation* of ideas should be permitted during the idea-production phase. Even though one may not accept brainstorming as a formal technique, it is useful to keep in mind the caution that premature evaluation can undermine and shut off good idea production.

The next stage of testing, evaluation, or forecasting of consequences is often a most difficult one, because it is not clear what criteria the group should be using to do its forecasting. As Wallen has pointed out,[1] testing criteria include (1) personal experience, (2) expert opinion, (3) surveying

1   Unpublished notes.

of existing data or information, and/or (4) planned scientific tests or research.

Personal experience and expert opinion are the easiest to obtain but the least valid. Surveys and research are more valid but also more time-consuming and expensive. One of the key functions of the process consultant is to provide to the group this range of alternatives, to enable it to correctly match its validation method to the kind of idea it is trying to test. For example, if the group is trying to decide between two products to develop, it should probably do some market surveying. If the group is trying to decide whether to put surplus funds into capital expansion or investment programs, it should obtain advice from financial experts, and so on. All too often a group uses just one validation method, no matter what ideas are being evaluated.

At each stage of problem-solving the discussion may reveal new features which lead to a reformulation of the problem. For example, in testing the idea that a new advertising campaign is needed, it may be discovered, from examining existing information, that the advertising campaign was perfectly sound; this raises the question whether the initial formulation of the problem as "consumer sales resistance" was correct. The process consultant should help the group to recognize that this kind of recycling, from initial formulation through idea production and idea testing to reformulation of the problem, is a very sound way to solve the problem. Reassurance from the consultant is usually necessary until a group becomes experienced in sensing its own problem-solving cycle because of the tendency to believe that constant reformulation of the problem is merely wasting time.

Cycle 2

All of cycle 1 involves steps which occur in discussion and which do not involve commitment to action unless the group chooses to gather some additional data for idea evaluation. As the group reaches some consensus on a proposed solution and makes a decision to act, we go into cycle 2, or the action cycle. The making of the decision is not shown in the diagram, but is represented by the act of crossing the boundary between cycle 1 and cycle 2.

Though a decision has been made on a given proposal or idea for solution, the problem-solving process is far from finished. The group must then still plan a detailed course of action, must take action steps, and must provide for some method to determine whether the action steps are solving the problem or not. This last step should be thought out in advance: "What information should we be looking at to determine whether or not our action steps are achieving the desired results?"

At any of these stages, it is again possible for the group to discover that it had not formulated the problem correctly; hence it may revert back to cycle 1 for some new reformulation and idea proposing and testing. Again I want to underline that such recycling is entirely desirable and should not be considered a waste of time. It is far more costly to be working on the wrong problem and to discover this only after expensive action steps have been taken, than to make an initially greater effort to define the problem correctly. Yet, as a process consultant, I have found it difficult to get groups to go back to step 1 and ask themselves the questions: "Have we formulated the problem correctly? Are we working on the right thing?"

The phase of action planning can be treated as a new problem requiring its own problem formulation (i.e., what are our problems in implementing the proposal we have decided on?), idea production (i.e., what are some alternative ways to implement the proposal?), and idea testing (i.e., which of our alternatives is the best way to implement the proposal?). If these stages are short-circuited or avoided, it is quite possible that a good proposal will be inadequately carried out and the group will draw the erroneous conclusion that it was the proposal which was deficient, instead of recognizing the defect as insufficient action planning. Here again the role of the process consultant may well be to *slow the group down* sufficiently to make it recognize that action planning is itself a problem-solving process.

In many cases the second cycle is delegated to some other person or group. For example, the original problem-solving group decides "Let's beef up our advertising campaign." Once it has reached this decision, it orders the advertising department to increase advertising on certain products. The group then relaxes and reverts to watching sales figures. Is this a sound approach? The answer in many cases is "No."

The major problem, when different people or groups perform cycle 1 and cycle 2, is that the second person (or group) may neither understand clearly nor be particularly committed to the proposal or solution which the cycle-1 person (or group) has come up with. He has not struggled with the problem definition; he has not had a chance to see the reasons why other alternatives which may now occur to him have been rejected; and he may not feel that the general proposal given to him is clear enough to permit implementation. Equally inefficient is the case where a group delegates cycle 1 to a task force or a consulting organization and then waits for a proposal in writing. In nine cases out of ten, if the originating group has not involved itself in cycle 1 and if the task force has not thought through cycle 2, the second group will not like the proposal and will find an excuse to shelve it.

Given these kinds of problems, it is desirable to ensure a high degree of communication between cycle-1 and cycle-2 persons or groups. The ideal situation would, of course, be that they are the same problem-solving unit. If that is not possible, the cycle-1 unit should provide for an interim phase which permits the cycle-2 unit to be completely on board before the two units sever their communication link. One might bring the implementer into the problem-solving process at the earliest possible stage, or, at least, review completely with the implementer all the steps which the cycle-1 unit has gone through in its efforts to arrive at a proposal for solution. In such a review, the key process would be to permit the implementer to satisfy himself completely by asking as many questions as he would like concerning the reasons why certain other alternatives which might strike him as better ones were not selected. He should either get satisfactory answers, or the cycle-1 group should go back and review the additional alternatives brought up by the implementer.

A good problem-solving group will protect itself against communication breakdown at the implementation stage by consulting the implementers at the earliest stages of idea production. If all their ideas are inserted early, there is less likelihood of missing important alternatives, and less likelihood of choosing something which will not make any sense to, or may be misunderstood by, the implementer. The role of the process consultant here is to help the group understand how difficult it is to communicate a complex solution to an implementer, and to ensure this understanding early enough in the problem-solving process to institute protective measures against communication breakdown. And there is no better protective method than to involve the ultimate implementer in the problem-solving at the earliest possible stage.

GROUP DECISION-MAKING

One of the key steps in the problem-solving process is the making of decisions. Decisions are involved at every stage of the process, but are only highly visible in the transition from cycle 1 to cycle 2, where the problem-solving unit commits itself to trying out a proposal for action.

Prior to this step the group has had to decide when and where to meet, how to organize itself, how to allocate time, by what procedures or rules to run its discussion (e.g., with or without a formal chairman, with or without Roberts' Rules of Order, etc.), how to tell when the problem has been sufficiently well formulated to move on to idea production, and so on. Often group members do not recognize actions which the group takes to answer issues like the above as group decisions, but, in fact they are decisions, and they set the climate of the group. Therefore, they need to be examined very carefully.

In reviewing the different decision-making methods listed below, it is important that we do not quickly judge any one method as better than another.[2] Each has its use at the appropriate time, and each method has certain consequences for future group operations. The important point is for the group to understand these consequences well enough to be able to choose a decision-making method which will be appropriate to the amount of time available, the past history of the group, the kind of task being worked on, and the kind of climate the group wants to establish.

1. *Decision by Lack of Response ("Plop").* The commonest and perhaps least visible group decision-making method is that in which someone suggests an idea, and, before anyone else has said anything about it, someone else suggests another idea, until the group finds one it will act on. All the ideas which have been bypassed, have, in a sense been decided upon by the group. But the decision has been simply a common decision not to support it, making the proposer feel that his suggestion has "plopped." The floors of most group meeting rooms are completely covered with plops.

2. *Decision by Authority Rule.* Many groups set up a power structure or start with a power structure which makes it clear that the chairman or someone in authority will make the decisions. The group can generate ideas and hold free discussion, but at any time the chairman can say that, having heard the discussion, he has decided to do thus and so. This method is highly efficient. Whether or not it is effective depends a great deal upon whether the chairman is a sufficiently good listener to have culled the right information on the basis of which to make his decision. Furthermore, if the group must move on to the next stage or implement the decision, the

2   The particular classification used here is patterned after a formulation first proposed by Robert Blake.

authority-rule method produces a minimum amount of involvement of the group. Hence it undermines the potential quality of the implementation of the decision.

I have often sat in meetings where the chairman has decided something after listening to the group for a few minutes, but where the action taken proved to be somehow out of line with what the chairman wanted. Upon later reconstruction it turned out that the group either misunderstood the decision or did not agree with it in the first place, and hence was neither able nor motivated to carry it out effectively.

3. *Decision by Minority.* One of the commonest complaints of group members is that they "feel railroaded" in reference to some decision. Usually this feeling results from one, two, or three people employing tactics which produce action and therefore must be considered decisions, but which are taken without the consent of the majority.

A single person can "railroad" a decision, particularly if he is in some kind of chairmanship role, by not giving opposition an opportunity to build up. Let us take an example pertaining to a decision as to how the group should work. The chairman says: "I think the way to go at this is to each state our opinion on the topic to see where we all stand. Now my own opinion is . . ." Once he has given his own opinion, he turns to the man on his right and says; "What do you think, Harry. . . . ?" When Harry has spoken, the chairman points to the next man and the group is off, having made in effect a decision about how it is going to go about its work. Yet *no one* agreed to this method of work, except the initiator. Another similar tactic is to say, "Well, we all seem to be agreed, so let's go ahead with John's idea," even though the careful observer may have detected that only John, the chairman, and maybe one other person has spoken favorably about the idea. The others have remained silent. If the chairman is asked how he concluded there was agreement, chances are that he will say, "Silence means consent, doesn't it? Everyone had a chance to voice opposition." If the group members are interviewed later, it sometimes is discovered that an actual majority was against John's idea, but that each one hesitated to speak up because he thought that all the other silent ones were for it. They too were trapped by "silence means consent."

Finally, a common form of minority rule is for two or more members to come to quick and powerful agreement on a course of action, to challenge the group with a quick "Does anyone object?", and, if no one raises his voice in two seconds, to proceed with "Let's go ahead, then." Again the trap is the assumption that silence means consent.

The process consultant plays an important role with respect to these first three decision-making methods primarily because they are rarely labeled as decision-making methods in the first place. Yet a great many group decisions, particularly pertaining to the important issue of group procedures, rules of order, and the like, are made in these rather rapid ways. For a group member to challenge such proceedings, to say "We don't really agree," is often seen as blocking; hence there are strong pressures on group members to stay silent and let things take their course, even though they are not in agreement.

The process consultant must first make the group aware of decisions which it has made and the methods by which it has made them; then he must try to get the group to assess whether they feel that these methods were appropriate to the situation. For example, the members might well agree that the chairman did railroad the decision, but they feel that this was appropriate because they were short of time, and knew that someone needed to make that decision quickly so that the group could get on with more important things.

On the other hand, the group might decide that a decision such as having each person in turn state his point of view introduces an element of formality and ritual into the group which undermines its ability to build creatively on ideas already advanced. The group might then wish to choose a different method of idea production. The important thing is to legitimize such process discussion and to have some observations available in case the group is finding it difficult to discern what the consultant is talking about. The principle of having the group attempt to generate its own observations first still applies, however.

4. *Decision by Majority Rule: Voting and/or Polling.* We come next to more familiar decision-making procedures, those which are often taken for granted as applying to any group situation because they reflect our political system. One simple version is to poll everyone's opinion following some period of discussion, and, if some majority feels the same way, to assume that that is the decision. The other method is the more formal one of stating a clear alternative and asking for votes in favor of it, votes against it, and abstentions.

On the surface this method seems completely sound, but surprisingly often it turns out that decisions made by this method are not well implemented even by the group that made the decision. What is wrong? If one can get the group to discuss its process, or if one interviews members of the minority, it turns out that two kinds of psychological barriers exist.

1. The minority member often feels that there was an insufficient period of discussion for him to really get his point of view across; hence he feels misunderstood and sometimes resentful;

2. The minority member often feels that the voting has created two camps within the group, that these camps are now in win-lose competition, that his camp lost the first round but that it is just a matter of time until it can regroup, pick up some support, and win the next time a vote comes up.

In other words, voting creates coalitions, and the preoccupation of the losing coalition is not how to implement what the majority wants, but how to win the next battle.

If voting is to be used, the group must be sure that it has created a climate in which members feel they have had their day in court, and where members feel obligated to go along with the majority decision. A key role for the process consultant is to highlight for the group what the pitfalls of each method are and to get enough discussion of group climate to ensure that the group will choose an appropriate decision-making strategy.

5. *Decision by Consensus.* One of the most effective but also most time-consuming methods of group decision-making is to seek consensus. It is important to understand that consensus, as I will define it, is not the same thing as unanimity. Rather, it is a state of affairs where communications have been sufficiently open, and the group climate has been sufficiently supportive, to make everyone in the group feel that he has had his fair chance to influence the decision. Someone then tests for the "sense of the meeting," carefully avoiding formal procedures like voting. If there is a clear alternative which most members subscribe to, and if those who oppose it feel they have had their chance to influence, then a consensus exists. Operationally it would be defined by the fact that those members who would not take the majority alternative, nevertheless understand it clearly and are prepared to support it. It is a psychological state which might be described as follows:

> "I understand what most of you would like to do. I personally would not do that, but I feel that you understand what my alternative would be. I have had sufficient opportunity to sway you to my point of view but clearly have not been able to do so. Therefore, I will gladly go along with what most of you wish to do."

In order to achieve such a condition, time must be allowed by the group for all members to state their opposition and to state it fully enough to get the feeling that others really do understand them. This condition is essential if they are later to free themselves of the preoccupation that they could have gotten their point of view across if others had only understood what they *really* had in mind. Only by careful listening to the opposition can such feelings be forestalled, and effective group decisions reached.

The process consultant can help the group to determine what kinds of decisions should be made by consensus. Which decisions are important enough to warrant the effort? One guideline he might suggest is that procedural decisions, those which pertain to *how* the group works, are the ones where it is most important that everyone be on board; hence these should probably be made by consensus. The group might decide to give complete authority to the chairman, or it might decide to try for very informal discussion procedures, or it might wish to brainstorm some ideas. But whatever is decided, it should be completely clear to everyone, and there should not be residual feelings of being misunderstood or desires to sabotage the group procedure. Unfortunately, this is the kind of decision that most often is made by minorities, costing the group untold hours of wasted effort because of low morale, lack of involvement, and lack of clarity in communication.

6. *Decision by Unanimous Consent.* The logically perfect but least attainable kind of decision is where everyone truly agrees on the course of action to be taken. For certain key kinds of decisions it may be necessary to seek unanimity, but for most important ones consensus is enough, if it is real consensus. The process consultant can help the group here by pointing out that the group may be setting *too high* a standard for itself in some cases. Unanimity is not always necessary, and may be a highly inefficient way to make decisions. The important thing is to take some time to agree on which method to use for what kinds of tasks and in what kinds of situations.

A Final Thought

Often the method of decision making is simply announced to the group by the convener or chairman. If this is the case, the process consultant must try to determine whether or not the group is comfortable with the method being used, and, if not, must find an opportunity to raise with the chairman the issue of whether he should permit some discussion by the group of how to handle the decision-making area. In my experience, chairmen often tend to feel threatened by such discussion because they fear that they will lose control of the group, and that disorder and chaos will result. One way to reassure them is by pointing out that different ways of making decisions do not necessarily imply a disorderly communication process. If the process consultant can provide some viable alternatives, he can often get the chairman to experiment with different methods, and draw his own conclusions.

SUMMARY

Problem-solving can be thought of as consisting of two cycles, one of which involves primarily discussion and the other primarily action-taking. The first cycle consists of the phases of problem identification and formulation, idea or proposal generation, and idea or proposal testing through attempting to forecast consequences. The most difficult stage is that of identifying and formulating what is really the problem; often this stage requires additional diagnostic effort.

The second cycle involves action planning, action steps, and evaluation of outcomes. The action planning is itself a problem-solving process and should be treated as such. The major difficulty in the total cycle is making the transition from cycle 1 to cycle 2 if different parties are involved. Those who have to implement the decisions should be involved in making them at the earliest possible stage.

The decision process itself can be handled by

1. lack of group response;

2. authority rule;

3. minority rule;

4. majority rule;

5. consensus; and/or

6. unanimity.

It is important for a group to become aware of these different decision-making methods and to learn to choose an appropriate method for the kind of task or decision it is working on.

6
GROUP NORMS AND GROUP GROWTH

GROUP NORMS

An important area for process observation is the kind of norms which develop in a group and the incidents around which norms develop. Norms are not easy to define or to identify in group process, yet they are very influential in determining member behavior and feelings, and part of this influence derives from their relative "invisibility."

A norm can be defined as a set of assumptions or expectations held by the members of a group or organization concerning what kind of behavior is right or wrong, good or bad, appropriate or inappropriate, allowed or not allowed. Norms are usually not articulated spontaneously, but members can state them if they are asked to. For example, some norms might be stated as follows:

"We should not swear or use foul language in this group."
"We should get to meetings on time."
"We should not challenge or question the statements of the chairman of the group."
"We should be informal with each other."
"Everyone in the group should participate and make a contribution."
"We should reach consensus and not fall back on voting."
"We should not start the meeting until all the members are present."

Those norms which are open, verbalized, or even written down function as the rules and regulations of the group and can for this purpose be called *explicit* norms. Those which are unspoken can be thought of as *implicit* norms. We know they are there from observing member reactions when they are violated: shocked silence, rebuke, Dutch-uncle talks, and the like.

Norms are powerful controls on our behavior. If they are violated, members are rebuked, punished in subtle ways, and ultimately ostracized or expelled from the group.

How do norms come about? One of the key sources of norms is our past experience in groups. We bring this past experience into the present and make the assumption that present groups should function more or less by the same rules as our past groups have. If past experience does not offer guidelines for the present situation, norms tend to form around the handling of critical incidents. For example, let us assume that one of the members strongly challenges the authority of the chairman by complaining about the manner in which the group is being run. An incident has been created. What the group does in the next few moments will determine to a large extent its future norms about handling authority. If the chairman fights back and the group supports him either by joining in the rebuke to the challenger or by remaining silent, a norm has been formed that "we don't challenge the authority of the chairman." If, on the other hand, the chairman permits the challenge and encourages others to voice their opinions, a norm has been formed that "we talk openly in the group about authority issues."

The process consultant can help the group by observing closely how critical incidents are handled, and by trying to infer the kinds of norms which the group is building for itself. If the group later engages in some process analysis of its own, the consultant can help the group to identify and reconstruct its own norms, and to test for itself whether or not the norms are helpful or constitute a barrier to effective action. For example, a group may discover that it has built up a norm of people speaking only when called on for an opinion. The group may feel that this formal mode of operation is getting in the way of good idea production. Having identified the norm, the group can then set about to change it explicitly to bring it into line with their feelings about how the group should operate.

The group may also discover that explicit and implicit norms tend to counteract each other. For example, there may be an explicit norm to say exactly what is on your mind, but an implicit norm that one must not contradict the ideas of certain powerful people in the group; there may be an explicit norm that all members of the group are equal and have an equal voice in the discussion, but an implicit norm that higher-status people in the group should speak first and that others should try to go along with their point of view. Norms such as this can be very subtle in their operation, and the process consultant must be able to identify concrete examples if the group is to learn to observe the effects of such norms for itself.

CRITERIA FOR GROUP GROWTH

Relationships and groups do develop and grow from early stages of "getting acquainted" to mature stages of effective, smooth functioning. It is often difficult, however, for a group to realize that it has developed and grown, because the criteria of growth are usually not well defined. The observer-consultant can be most helpful in identifying for the group some of the ways in which it has developed and matured.

There is no single criterion which can be universally applied to test the degree of maturity of a group, but there are a number of dimensions along which the group can assess itself in order to identify where it has grown and where it may still need further development. These dimensions can be put into a simple self-rating questionnaire which the members can fill out periodically to determine how they feel about each dimension and how these feelings change over time. A sample of such a questionnaire is shown in Figure 6.1.

The dimensions shown in the questionnaire derive from some basic criteria of maturity which parallel criteria developed for individual maturity. These can be stated as follows:

1. Does the group have the capacity to deal realistically with its environment and is it independent of its environment to an optimal degree?

2. Is there a basic agreement within the group about ultimate goals and values?

3. Is there in the group a capacity for self-knowledge? Does the group understand why it does what it does?

4. Is there an optimum use of the resources available within the group?

5. Does the group have the capacity to learn from its experience? Can it assimilate new information and respond flexibly to it?

A MATURE GROUP POSSESSES:

1. Adequate mechanisms for getting feedback:

   Poor feedback   1 2 3 4 5   Excellent feedback
   mechanisms   Average   mechanisms

2. Adequate decision making procedure:

   Poor decision   1 2 3 4 5   Very adequate deci-
   making procedure   Average   sion making

3. Optimal cohesion:

   Low cohesion   1 2 3 4 5   Optimal cohesion
                         Average

4. Flexible organization and procedures:

   Very inflexible   1 2 3 4 5   Very flexible
                         Average

5. Maximum use of member resources:

   Poor use of   1 2 3 4 5   Excellent use of
   resources   Average   resources

6. Clear communications:

   Poor communi-   1 2 3 4 5   Excellent communication   Average   cation

7. Clear goals accepted by members:

   Unclear goals—   1 2 3 4 5   Very clear goals—
   not accepted   Average   accepted

8. Feelings of interdependence with authority persons:

   No interdepen-   1 2 3 4 5   High interdependence   Average   dence

9. Shared participation in leadership functions:

   No shared   1 2 3 4 5   High shared
   participation   Average   participation

10. Acceptance of minority views and persons:

    No acceptance   1 2 3 4 5   High acceptance
                         Average

Fig. 6.1 Criteria of group maturity.

6. Is there an integration of the group's internal processes—communication, decision-making, distribution of authority and influence, and norms?

No group is going to achieve some perfect level on all of these dimensions. The major usefulness of the dimensions is that they permit the group to study its own progress over time and to identify weak spots in its operation. They also enable the group to gain confidence by noting progress along one or more dimensions. As I stated above, the process consultant can often help best by noting and reporting such progress to the group.

SUMMARY

The origin, function, and meaning of group norms were discussed. I tried to highlight the importance which norms have in the life of the group, making norms and their formation one of the key things for the process consultant to keep close track of. Some dimensions or criteria for the growth and development of a group were also discussed, and a special role for the consultant identified as encouraging a group to analyze how it had grown, since this process is often invisible to the group members.

7

LEADERSHIP AND AUTHORITY

The area of leadership and authority serves as a kind of bridge between group processes and intergroup or organizational processes. Managers have the power not only to influence what goes on in their immediate interpersonal surroundings, but to set up organizational structures and reward systems which will determine a whole variety of other process events such as who communicates with whom, who feels cooperative and who feels competitive, how motivated subordinates down the line will be, and so on.

MANAGERIAL ASSUMPTIONS

In my book *Organizational Psychology,* I identified four basic sets of assumptions which have been reflected in managerial theory and which determine managerial or leadership behavior:

1. *Rational-economic Man.* This set of assumptions, closely paralleling McGregor's Theory X, is built on the view that man works for money, that he must be motivated and controlled by economic incentives, and that, being lazy, without managerial effort he would basically do nothing. Therefore, the leader must motivate, must organize, must control, and, in effect, must bear the responsibility and burden of his subordinates' performance.

2. *Social Man.* This set of assumptions is built on the view that man's basic needs are to have good relationships with both fellow workers and supervisors. The leader must therefore set up a congenial work situation, must care about his men, must understand their needs and go to bat for them, and must establish close and harmonious relations with them.

3. *Self-actualizing Man.* This set of assumptions is built on the view that man has a hierarchy of needs and, as lower-order needs are satisfied, higher-order needs come into play, culminating in man's need to use all of his potential and thereby to "actualize" himself. The leader must therefore provide adequate challenge, a work situation which permits subordinates to use their talents fully, and enough understanding of his men to know when and how to challenge them. There is no need to control and motivate men. The motivation is already there waiting to be released and the capacity for self-control is also already present within man. This set of assumptions is closely parallel to McGregor's Theory Y.

4. *Complex Man.* This set of assumptions is built on the view that men are different from each other and that they change and grow in their motives as well as in knowledge and skills. Therefore, a man can start out being rational-economic but can learn to be self-actualizing. It will depend upon the organization, his personality, and a whole host of other factors. The leader must be a good diagnostician in order to know what the motivations and abilities of his subordinates actually are, and must be flexible enough to provide different kinds of leadership for different people.

The process consultant often has the opportunity to observe a manager in action. He can see him handle people, run groups, issue written memoranda, and think out loud. One way the consultant can attempt to interpret what he hears and observes is to ask himself what underlying assumptions about people the manager holds, and how these assumptions are in turn influencing the manager's leadership style. As opportunities arise to discuss issues, the consultant can then direct the manager's thinking to his own assumptions. The consultant can provide observations and help the manager to interpret the implications of his own behavior.

For example, I have spent some time with a manager who told me that he wants his immediate subordinates to take more initiative in running their own operations. A little while later he showed me a list of nineteen (!!) questions which he had asked of one of these subordinates about a proposal which this particular person had made. I asked the manager whether he thought there was any inconsistency between the messages he was sending to his subordinate: "Take more initiative" and, at the same time, "Here are nineteen things you had better think about before you act."

After some further exploration, it turned out that the manager really didn't trust his subordinates to the extent he professed. His elaborate questioning attitude was a clear signal of this mistrust. Consequently subordinates behaved very cautiously. Only after some real exploration of his own behavior did the manager realize that ideally he wanted initiative, but in practice he wanted pretty tight control. Once he recognized these feelings in himself he became less upset over the cautious behavior of his subordinates.

Another example illustrates a more far-reaching organizational phenomenon. A company president who prides himself on creating a climate in which engineers and other professionals really feel challenged by their work was told that the company's internal communications system was being overused and costing too much. He verified the fact of the high costs and then instructed his office manager to issue a memorandum which turned out to be very punitive and rather supercilious in its tone. It was as if it had been written either for very stupid or very recalcitrant people. The president asked me what I thought of it, prior to his sending it out.

The ensuing discussion was aimed at helping this man see the inconsistency between a climate in which people were treated as professionals and a memorandum which treated them as if they were recalcitrant children. I argued that if the memorandum went out in its original form, the communications system might indeed be used less but the climate of professionalism might be irreparably damaged. The president would be sending out a message which implied that he didn't really trust his people at all, something which would have been quite inconsistent with his actual feelings. Being unused to thinking in terms of total organizational effects of managerial communications, he did not initially see the inconsistency. Once he saw it, he could choose the kind of message he was willing to have go out to his organization.

Many managers are, of course, truly ambivalent. They want to trust people and they send signals accordingly; at the same time they are afraid to trust them and unwittingly send out other signals which imply mistrust. The process consultant can help best by encouraging self-examination, so that the ambivalence itself comes to be recognized as a real feeling. The manager can then choose whether to lean in one direction or the other, or to continue to be ambivalent. But whatever course he now chooses, he does so with some insight into the probable effects of his behavior on the people around him.

STYLES OF DECISION-MAKING

We have previously referred to the different means by which *groups* make decisions. Looking at this process from the perspective of the manager, we can now analyze what options are open to him when he must initially structure an interpersonal situation. This issue applies to staff meetings, to task forces, or to any kind of situation where some people are brought together for the eventual solution of a problem. The most useful formulation of the action alternatives available to the manager has been provided by Tannenbaum and Schmidt (1958). They identify a basic dimension which runs from *total leader autocracy* on one end to *total group autonomy* on the other end (see Fig. 7.1). At one extreme the leader makes the decision and simply announces it to the others involved; at the other extreme the leader states the ultimate target to be achieved but gives the group complete freedom in how to achieve it.

Most managers recognize these extremes readily. What they are less likely to recognize is that there are a number of in-between positions and that the leader can choose different positions at different times. For example, he can make the decision himself but make a real effort to explain and sell it to others. He can retain the power to make the decision but can tell the group what his ideas are and invite comment prior to making the decision. Still further along on the continuum, he can present the problem and invite ideas and alternatives from the group prior to making a decision, or he can let the group know of several alternatives among which they might choose. He can state some limits outside of which the group may not go, but permit the group to decide within those limits. And he can vary his behavior from one decision to the next.

What factors will determine the appropriate position for any given managerial situation? Tannenbaum and Schmidt identify three sets of forces which should be considered:

1. forces in the leader himself;

2. forces in the subordinates; and

3. forces in the situation.

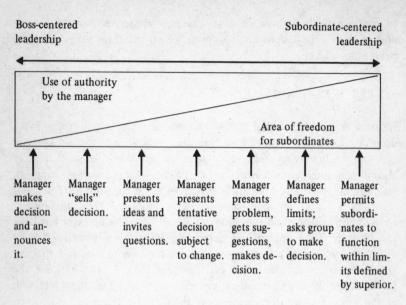

Fig. 7.1 A continuum of leadership behavior.*

The forces in the leader are things like his value system, his confidence in the group, his own natural inclinations or style, and the security he feels in the situation. Forces in the group would be things like their prior experience in making decisions, their actual competence, their tolerance for ambiguity, their ability to become involved in the problem, and their expectations and need for growth. Forces in the situation would be things like the amount of time pressure, the type of problem which is to be solved, and the type of organization in which the process is occurring.

The process consultant can be most useful in helping the manager see the alternatives available to him and in helping him make a diagnosis of the various forces which have been outlined. There are no right or wrong assumptions about people in the abstract and there is no right or wrong leadership style in the abstract. The problem for the manager is to make an accurate diagnosis and to choose a course of action appropriate to that diagnosis.

---

*   Tannenbaum, R., and Schmidt, H. W., "How to choose a leadership pattern." *Harv. Bus. Rev.*, March-April, 1958.

It should be noted that the kind of leadership/managership theory which I am espousing says relatively little about the traits or characteristics of the leader. I do not believe that there is some magic set of traits which can be identified in all leaders, nor do I believe that all leadership/managerial situations call for the same mix of traits. The unique requirements for being a good president may be quite different from the requirements for a good vice-president. The production manager often has to be a very different type of person from a sales manager or a research manager. Each has to be a leader, but what he must do to lead effectively varies with the job and the situation.

Given the above ideas, the process consultant cannot really help a company to identify who should be in what job or who should be promoted. Indeed, his initial psychological contract with the organization would probably preclude involvement in such activities. On the other hand, the consultant might be most useful by helping a manager to think through whether his own traits, values, motives, and temperament are suited for a particular kind of leadership position he is in or aspires to be in. If he has observed the manager in action, he can certainly provide observations which may help the manager to think more clearly about his own style and to select a leadership pattern which fits him best. If he finds incompatibilities between job demands and his personal style, he can then, on his own, seek a niche where his style matches job requirements better.

SUMMARY

Leadership or managership has been identified as a highly variable kind of behavior which depends upon the person, his subordinates, the nature of the job requirements, and the kind of problem situation to be dealt with. Therefore, no easy generalizations can be made about leadership. Two ways of increasing understanding about leader behavior were discussed. One, the kinds of underlying assumptions which the person makes about people will determine how he will lead or manage them. Becoming aware of one's own assumptions is therefore crucial. Two, the leader has a number of choices of how tightly to centralize control and how flexible to be from one decision to the next. By diagnosing forces in himself, in his subordinates, and in the situation, he can increase his flexibility and thereby his effectiveness.

8
INTERGROUP PROCESSES

One of the most important and least studied aspects of organizational process is intergroup relations within an organization. It is no longer an issue whether or not groups form in organizations. The evidence is overwhelming that they do—along formal departmental lines, along geographical lines, and in terms of who has to interact with whom in the course of getting the work done. It is also well known that groups develop norms, that members feel loyal to their groups and adopt the norms, and that the goals of different groups sometimes run at cross-purposes with each other.

What is relatively less well known are the consequences of such group behavior in terms of costs or benefits to the organization as a whole. For example, many managers will argue that they want various departments to compete with each other because it improves the level of motivation of each group. Other managers will argue that they cannot afford to have departments compete with each other because if they did they would not produce the best possible joint product. I have heard still other managers argue that groups do not have any significant effect on motivation, productivity, or morale, and hence can be discounted.

STUDYING GROUP PROCESSES

Part of the problem of making sense of this area is that the key processes are relatively invisible. If the engineering department has poor relations with the production department, the production men might be motivated *not* to correct errors which they find in the drawings given to them; without the excuse of ignorance, therefore, they deliberately produce bad products. The ultimately bad product is visible enough, but the lack of interest on the part of the production worker (who failed to correct what he knew was a fault) is hard to observe; it is a private decision on his part *not* to do something. Similarly, the giving of false information or the withholding of information, which typically results from groups competing with each other in a win-lose situation, is difficult to observe, even when one suspects strongly that it is there.

The process consultant can use a variety of techniques in an effort to learn about such intergroup processes.

1. He can interview members of each group about their feelings toward the other group and can inquire how they translate these feelings into overt behavior.

2. He can try to observe meetings or settings where members of both groups are present and assess the degree of openness of communication, spirit of cooperation, etc.

3. He can try to theorize what should happen between the groups and check his theories by observing specific situations. For example, if relationships are good, he would theorize that errors by one group would be sympathetically and helpfully dealt with by the other group. He can then try to find an incident where an error occurred and either observe what happens, or, if the incident is past, ask what happened at the time.

4. A final and more complicated method for assessing and working on intergroup process is to arrange an intergroup exercise of some sort. One model which was developed by Robert Blake involves the following steps:

a) Each group separately describes its own image of itself and its image of the other group.

b) Through representatives these images are then reported by each group to the other. Both groups now have some new data about how they are perceived by each other.

c) The next stage is not to react, but to meet separately to consider what kind of behavior on the part of each group may have led to the image which the other group holds.

d)   These behavioral hypotheses are then shared and discussed openly by both groups.

e)   In the final stage the groups work together toward reducing the discrepancy between self-image and the image held by the other group, by planning how to relate differently toward each other in future contacts.

If this process is used it brings both groups into the common task of exploring why discrepancies of perceptions exist, and thus reduces the competitive task each group faces in trying to outdo the other group and show up well with the rest of the organization or higher-level authorities.

It is particularly important for the high-level manager to understand intergroup processes because he often has the choice of whether to reward competition, collaboration, or complete independence. Since the commonest tendency appears to be to arrange competitive conditions, the process consultant must often attempt to get across some of the possible consequences of competition *before* the win-lose situation arises. These consequences have been derived from laboratory and field experiments and can be reliably reproduced in exercises which involve two groups in win-lose competition.

Before a decision is reached what happens within and between the competing groups?

What Happens Within Each Competing Group?

1. Each group becomes more closely knit and elicits greater loyalty from its members; members close ranks and bury some of their internal differences.

2. Group climate changes from informal, casual, playful, to work- and task-oriented; concern for members' psychological needs declines while concern for task accomplishment increases.

3. Leadership patterns tend to change from more democratic toward more autocratic; the group becomes more willing to tolerate autocratic leadership.

4. Each group becomes more highly structured and organized.

5. Each group demands more loyalty and conformity from its members in order to be able to present a "solid front."

What Happens Between the Competing Groups?

1. Each group begins to see the other groups as the enemy, rather than merely a neutral object.

2. Each group begins to experience distortions of perception: it tends to perceive only the best parts of itself, denying its weaknesses, and tends to perceive only the worst parts of the other group, denying its strengths. Each group is likely to develop a negative stereotype of the other ("they don't play fair the way we do").

3. Hostility toward the other group increases while interaction and communication with the other group decrease; thus it becomes easier to maintain negative stereotypes and more difficult to correct perceptual distortions.

4. If the groups are forced into interaction—for example, if they are forced to listen to representatives plead their own and the others' cause in reference to some task—each group is likely to listen more closely to their own representative and not to listen to the representative of the other group, except to find fault with his presentation; in other words, group members tend to listen only for that which supports their own position and stereotype.

After a decision has been rendered what happens to the winner and loser?

What happens to the winner?

1. Winner retains its cohesion and may become even more cohesive.

2. Winner tends to release tension, lose its fighting spirit, become complacent, casual, and playful (the "fat and happy" state).

3. Winner tends toward high intragroup cooperation and concern for members' needs, and low concern for work and task accomplishment.

4. Winner tends to be complacent and to feel that winning has confirmed the positive stereotype of itself and the negative stereotype of the "enemy" group; there is little basis for reevaluating perceptions, or reexamining group operations in order to learn how to improve them.

What happens to the loser?

1. If the situation permits because of some ambiguity in the decision (say, if judges have rendered it or if the game was close), there is a

strong tendency for the loser to deny or distort the reality of losing; instead, the loser will find psychological escapes like "the judges were biased," "the judges didn't really understand our solution," "the rules of the game were not clearly explained to us," "if luck had not been against us at the one key point, we would have won," and so on.

2. If the defeat is accepted, the losing group tends to splinter, unresolved conflicts come to the surface, and fights break out, all in the effort to find a cause for the loss.

3. Loser is more tense, ready to work harder, and desperate to find someone or something to blame—the leader, the group itself, the judges who decided against them, the rules of the game (the "lean and hungry" state).

4. Loser tends toward low intragroup cooperation, low concern for members' needs, and high concern for recouping by working harder.

5. Loser tends to learn a lot about itself as a group because the positive stereotype of itself and the negative stereotype of the other group are upset by the loss, forcing a reevaluation of perceptions; as a consequence, the loser is likely to reorganize and become more cohesive and effective, once the loss has been accepted realistically.

It is far easier to prevent reactions and feelings such as these by not arranging a competitive reward structure in the first place, than it is to undo them once they have become established. The process consultant must find ways of bringing relevant data to the attention of the manager so that he can see for himself that a motivational system which seems sound can have pitfalls in it. If the situation has become competitive and destructive, remedial measures such as those mentioned at the beginning of this chapter may have to be tried.

OTHER ORGANIZATIONAL PROCESSES.

The process consultant finds himself, through his observation of managerial behavior, witness to a variety of other organizational processes besides the ones we have looked at. For example, he sees how managerial decisions in the areas of accounting, budgeting, and controlling will signal to the organization the degree to which subordinates are or are not trusted. The manner in which managers administer performance-appraisal plans or bonus plans also communicates a great deal about their assumptions, and therefore has an immediate as well as long-range effect on the organization. The kind of career planning which is done, the use of training or development activities, the policies for recruitment and job placement, all have implications for how people will feel, how they will relate to each other, and how they will carry out their work.

It is beyond the scope of this volume to treat each of these process areas in detail. For the present I merely wish to note that there are a variety of other processes to which the consultant must pay attention and which he must assess if he is to help the organization become more effective. I have deliberately concentrated on the more immediate kinds of process which one sees in face-to-face relations because these are the most accessible and the most likely to produce important behavior change. If organization members can change their behavior in their immediate relations, this will inevitably produce more far-reaching effects organizationally. Even more important, if managers can learn how to diagnose organizational processes better, they can continue to modify their behavior after the consultant is no longer present.

SUMMARY

We have looked briefly at some intergroup and total organizational processes. Of especial importance are the conditions which are set up for groups within organizations leading to competition or collaboration. The problems of internal competition were spelled out, and it was noted how much more difficult it is to undo these effects than to avoid them in the first place. The process consultant must play an active role in encouraging managers to think through their approach to intergroup relations.

PART 2
INTERVENTION

So far in this book I have concentrated on the *diagnosis* of organizational process. In providing examples, I have referred to some of the kinds of process interventions which the consultant can make. In Part 2 of this book I would like to reverse the focus and concentrate primarily on the strategy and tactics of *intervention,* with the diagnostic focus being secondary. In other words, how and by what criteria does the process consultant enter and manage a relationship with his client, and what action steps can he and does he take to achieve the goals of the consultation process?

In answering these kinds of questions I will draw more heavily on case examples from my own consulting experience, and will give as much detailed case information as I can. In order to maintain confidentiality, I have disguised the identities of the clients, but have tried to preserve the essence of what was going on. As the reader will note, the area of intervention and the criteria for managing a client-consultant relationship are not nearly as well worked out as the areas of interpersonal behavior and group functioning which have been previously discussed. I will try to be as open as I can be about what actually were my criteria for action, but these criteria should *not,* at this stage of the development of the field, be viewed as general principles.

THE STAGES OF PROCESS CONSULTATION

We may list the stages of a process-consultation cycle as follows, but we must recognize that they interact and overlap with each other.

1. Initial contact with the client organization;

2. Defining the relationship, formal contract, and psychological contract;

3. Selecting a setting and a method of work;

4. Data gathering and diagnosis;

5. Intervention;

6. Reducing involvement;

7. Termination.

It must be emphasized that these stages are not very easily defined in terms of periods of time. Rather they are logically distinct areas which the consultant must work on. Some of the stages (for example, diagnosis and intervention) go on simultaneously. Some stages, like defining the psychological contract, are perpetual in the sense that they are constantly being reviewed and revised.

In Chapter 9, I will discuss the manner in which initial contact is made between the client organization and the consultant, and how this leads to an exploratory meeting of some sort. Many consultation efforts terminate at this stage because either the organization or the consultant does not wish to pursue matters. During the exploratory meeting the main work is to begin to establish a relationship and to define both a formal and a psychological contract. If a satisfactory initial relationship is formed, the process continues with the selection of a setting and a method of work. This process will be discussed in Chapter 10.

Chapter 11 will focus on some of the methods by which the consultant gathers data in trying to develop a diagnosis of what is going on, and Chapter 12 will discuss in detail some of the methods of intervention which are available to the consultant. Though these chapters imply that diagnosis and intervention are separate processes, it must never be forgotten that every diagnostic step is an intervention of some sort, and every intervention reveals further data. The separation of these stages is therefore a purely conceptual one.

Chapter 13 will deal with the problem of how to reduce involvement and terminate a relationship when the consultation process is no longer serving a useful function for the client system. In Chapter 14, I will try to summarize and lay out some issues for the future.

9

ESTABLISHING CONTACT
AND DEFINING A RELATIONSHIP

INITIAL CONTACT WITH THE CLIENT SYSTEM

Initial contact is made when someone from the client organization (contact client) telephones or writes me about some problem which he is experiencing or which he perceives in some part of his organization. Usually he comes to me for one of a number of reasons:

a) he has heard somewhere a talk I have given on a topic related to his perceived problem;

b) he has read a paper or book I have written which deals with the general area he is concerned about;

c) he has become acquainted with me during a training program or group-dynamics laboratory;

d) he has been referred to me by a colleague who was approached on the basis of (a), (b), or (c) and who could not undertake the project; or

e) he has been referred by someone else in his own organization or some other manager who is acquainted with me in some way.

The contact client indicates that he perceives a problem which he feels is not being solved by normal organizational procedures, or he sees a lack which cannot be filled by normal organizational resources.

For example, in Case A, the Apex Manufacturing Company, the contact client was a divisional manager one level below the president. The company is a large manufacturing concern, organized into several divisions. The contact client indicated that there were communication problems in the top management group resulting from a recent reorganization. Because the company expected to grow rapidly in the next several years, they felt they should work on these kinds of problems now.

In Case B, the Boyd Consumer Goods Company, the contact client was a member of the personnel department who had known of my interests for some time, had had other contacts with professors at the Sloan School (M.I.T.), and was interested in finding a consultant to help the newly appointed president manage the transition from "traditional" to more "modern" techniques of management in his organization.

In Case C, the Central Chemical Company, a large multidivision chemical manufacturing concern, the contact client was a fellow faculty member at M.I.T., who had been working with the company and had learned that its management wished some additional consultation help in instituting a variety of change programs in several of their divisions. This company had originally become interested through reading and hearing Douglas McGregor, had built a strong internal personnel staff in one of the divisions, and had launched a number of very creative internal-change programs. The management felt that continual contact with outside resources would help the total effort.

In Case D, The Delta Manufacturing Company, a large manufacturer of consumer appliances, the contact client was a member of the company's central personnel staff. He had been working in one of the divisions helping various production groups in developing strong interpersonal collaboration and team spirit. When the division director became interested in a similar kind of activity for himself and his staff, he asked the inside man to find him a consultant who could work with the group.

In most such cases, I do not know from the initial contact what the real problem is, and therefore only agree to discuss it further at an exploratory meeting. If I have some consultation time available, I will schedule such a meeting in the near future. If I do not have time, I will either ask if the problem can wait or suggest someone else who might be able to help. Occasionally I will agree to an exploratory meeting with the understanding that if anything comes of it, the work would be done at a later time.

One of the most important criteria for predicting the likelihood that a useful consultation relationship will result is the initial relationship formed between contact client and consultant. I find that I evaluate the degree of openness, spirit of inquiry, and authenticity of communication of the contact client. For example, to evaluate openness, I try to assess the responses I get to some of my own questions. If I ask whether the caller is willing to sit down and explore things, I look for a response which indicates genuine willingness. If the caller seems too certain he already *knows* what is wrong; if he has me miscast as an expert in something which I am not expert in; or if he clearly has a misconception of behavioral science or organizational psychology,—these are all reasons for caution. If I feel the caller wants merely reassurance for some course of action he has already embarked on or wants a quick solution for a surface problem, I will be reluctant to proceed.

If none of the barriers described above arises, the exploratory meeting becomes the first major diagnostic step toward the establishment of a relationship. It should be noted that the kind of evaluation made by the process consultant requires that he be relatively indifferent about whether or not he ends up with a client. The commercial consultant is at a disadvantage because he is trying to sell his services. A process consultant should be free of this pressure, so that he can genuinely evaluate whether he can be helpful to the client or not. He should be free to turn down potential clients who would not benefit from the help.

As can be seen, process consultation cannot start until someone in the organization accepts the assumption that relationships and interpersonal processes are important targets for learning. Gaining entry to an organization in the role of a process consultant is, therefore, highly contingent upon one or more internal people who are willing to expose their processes to scrutiny. Often these people have only the vaguest ideas of what their problems are; but they sense that all is not as good as it could be and invite observation and comment. This spirit of inquiry is an essential characteristic of a potentially successful client-consultant relationship.

THE EXPLORATORY MEETING:
DEFINING THE FORMAL AND PSYCHOLOGICAL CONTRACT

The exploratory meeting usually involves the contact client, one or more of his associates, and the consultant. Usually the consultant and contact client have decided in a preliminary discussion at a prior time *which* other people should be at the meeting. The criteria for who should be present are difficult to define, but some preliminary ones that I think about and suggest to the contact client should be mentioned:

a) someone who is high enough in the organization to be able to influence others if he himself is influenced;

b) someone who is generally in tune with the idea of bringing in a consultant to help on organizational problems;

c) someone who sees specific problems which require working on;

d) someone who is familiar with behavioral-science consultants and the process-consultation idea.

One should avoid having anyone at these early meetings who is hostile, skeptical, or totally ignorant of the kinds of service which can be offered by the consultant. If one or more such people are present and challenge me to prove that I can be of help to them, we are no longer exploring the problem; instead I find myself seduced into a selling role. If I permit myself to get into this role, I am already violating the process-consultation model of helping others to help themselves. I may persuade them to use some other expert service of mine, but I cannot easily redefine my role as process consultant.[1]

The exploratory meeting is usually a long lunch or a half-day meeting. I usually mention to the contact client that the company should be prepared to pay a consultation fee for the exploratory meeting. The logic of this decision is that process consultation really starts with the initial contact. The kinds of diagnostic questions I ask, the frame of reference from which I approach the problem, the sorts of things I observe and react to, all constitute initial interventions which, to some degree, influence the client's perception of his own problem. After three or four hours of exploration of his company's problems, the contact client has new perspectives and new insights. At the same time I am sharing my scarcest resource—time.

The purposes of the exploratory meeting are:

a) to determine more precisely what the problem is,

b) to assess whether my involvement is likely to be of any help to the organization,

1   If the contact *starts* with members of the client system who are interested in trying process consultation, it is often possible at a later stage to design meetings or settings in which the resistant members of the system can be confronted and conflicts worked through.

c)   to assess whether the problem is going to be of interest to me,

d)   to formulate next action steps if the answers to (b) and (c) are positive.

These purposes are usually accomplished by a fairly open-ended discussion with the contact client. I usually ask questions which are designed to (1) sharpen and highlight aspects of the presented problem, and (2) test how open and frank the contact client is willing to be. If I feel that there is hedging, unwillingness to be critical of his own organization, confusion about his motives, and/or confusion about my potential role as consultant, I will be cautious. I will suggest that nothing should be decided without more exploration, or I will terminate the relationship if I am definitely pessimistic about establishing a good relationship.

For example, in Case A the contact client was a key manager immediately below the president. He spoke openly about his concerns that the president needed help in handling certain key people, shared his worries that the president and his key subordinates were not in good communication, and indicated that recent company history suggested the need for some stabilizing force in the organization. I asked him whether the president knew he had come to me and what the president's feelings were about bringing in a consultant. The contact client indicated that the president as well as other key executives were all in favor of bringing someone in to work with them. All saw the need for some outside help.

In Case B, the exploratory meeting was relatively perfunctory because I had already met the president at a management-development session run by the company some months earlier at which I was the speaker. The meeting consisted of the personnel vice-president, the president, and myself, and moved rapidly toward the next stage of actually defining the contract, the goals, and the setting in which to work.

In Case C, the fellow consultant who had recommended me acted as go-between and arranged a suitable set of goals and targets for my visit to the company. No contact with the company occurred except by some correspondence until my first visit.

In Case D, the exploratory meeting was a lunch with the division manager, the inside consultant, and myself. Our purpose was to determine whether the division manager and I would "hit it off together," whether we could agree on some reasonable goals for consultation, and how best to proceed if things looked promising.

In each of the above cases the initial exploration led to a favorable response on both my part and that of the contact client. To illustrate an unfavorable outcome, in Case E, the Etna Production Company, the contact client called me to meet with him and his key personnel group to evaluate a new performance-appraisal program they were planning to launch across the whole company. The contact client was the director of personnel. The exploratory meeting lasted one day, during which time company representatives outlined the proposed program. I questioned a number of points which seemed internally inconsistent and found the client becoming obviously defensive. The farther we went into the discussion, the clearer it became that the client was completely committed to his program and was seeking only reassurance from me. From the way in which he reacted to questions and criticisms, it became clear that he was not willing to reexamine any part of his program. He did not really want an evaluation; hence the relationship was terminated at the end of the one day.

I try to be as open and confronting as I can be during the exploratory meeting, partly as a test of how willing the client is to be open, and partly to make it clear from the outset how I would define my role as consultant. The most important point to get across is that I will not function as an expert problem-solver in the traditional consultation role; rather, I will attempt to intervene directly in organizational processes as I see the opportunity. This point has to be made explicit very early because the very entry of the consultant into the organization already constitutes an intervention of some magnitude. In other words, I would be deluding myself and the client if I said that I might or might not intervene. Rather, I have to get him to accept the idea that intervention is fundamental to consultation, but that the nature and degree of intervention is dependent upon joint diagnosis and joint decision between the client and myself.

If I feel that the contact client can accept the consultant as an intervener in organizational process, and if my relationship with the client is progressing comfortably during the exploratory meeting, the discussion usually moves toward the defining of the formal and psychological contract.

The contract. There are two aspects to the contract: One is the formal decision as to how much time will be devoted to consultation, what services will be performed, and what form and amount of payment will be used; the other aspect concerns the actual "psychological contract"—what the client basically expects to gain from the relationship, and what the consultant expects to gain. It is important for both client and consultant to explore both aspects of the contract, not just the formal ones.

On the formal side, I have a simple ground rule. I will work up to a certain number of days per month for a flat *per diem* fee. I do not wish the client organization to formally commit itself, nor do I wish to promise a continuing relationship. Both parties should be free to terminate the agreement at any time if the relationship is no longer satisfactory or useful. This mutual freedom to terminate is important to ensure that the basis of the relationship is the *actual value obtained,* not the fulfillment of some obligation entered into.

On the other hand, both the client and consultant should be prepared to give as much time to the project as is mutually agreed on as desirable. If I have only one day per month available, and the nature of the problem is such that more time may be needed by the client, I should obviously not begin the consultation in the first place. I try to make a reasonably good estimate of how much time the project might take if it goes well, and ensure that I have that much time available. For his part, the client should budget costs in such a way that if more days are needed, he has the resources to pay for them. In no case has anything of this sort ever been formalized beyond a letter of terms written by the client. Once we agree on the *per diem* rate, I keep records of the amount of time spent, and send monthly bills to the client.

On the psychological side, I try to assess as early in the relationship as possible all the expectations which may be deliberately or unwittingly concealed by the client. Beyond work on the presented problem, the client may have a variety of other expectations such as the following: The client may expect me to give him personal evaluations of people in his organization; he may expect me to tell him how to deal with "problem people" in his organization; he may expect me to give "expert" opinions on how he should handle management problems; he may expect me to lend support to some program or decision he has made which he is trying to sell to others; and so on. It is important that as many as possible of these expectations be revealed early, so that they don't function as traps or sources of disappointment later on if and when I refuse to go along with something which the client expects of me.

On my side, I have to be as clear as I can be in what I expect of the organization and of myself in my role as consultant. For example, I expect a willingness to diagnose and explore problem issues; I expect a willingness to take some time to find out what is going on rather than rushing in hastily; I expect to be supported in my suggestions as to *how* to gather data; I expect organization members to be committed to the project, and not to be dragging their feet or persisting in a veiled resistance.

I also have to state clearly what I will do and what I will not do. For example, I have to fully explain the idea that my client is not just the *contact person* or the person of highest rank, but the *entire group* with which I am working, and, by implication, the entire organization. In other words, I would not support decisions which I believed would harm the hourly employees even if I never talked to any of these employees.

This concept of the whole group or organization as the client is one of the trickiest yet most important aspects of process consultation. In observing other consulting firms operating in companies in which I have also been working, I have noticed that many of the best firms essentially take the president as their client, convince him regarding the program he should institute, and then proceed to help him to sell the program to others in the organization.

In contrast, as a process consultant I have found myself to be most effective if I can gain the trust of *all* key parties with whom I am working, so that none ever thinks of me as pushing someone else's ideas. I have found that this is quite possible to achieve across several levels of the organization. Indeed, in Case A, after many months of working with the president and his six key subordinates, I arrived at a point where all of them saw me as a potentially useful communication link. They asked me quite sincerely to report to each one the feelings or reactions of others whenever I learned anything I felt should be passed on. At the same time they were quite open with me about each other, knowing that I might well pass on any opinions or reactions they voiced to me. They did not want me to treat everything as confidential because they trusted me and each other enough.

This case was of great interest because of my own feeling that my having to serve as carrier of this type of information was not an ideal role for me, and reflected an insufficient ability on their part to tell each other things directly. Hence I took two courses of action. First, I tried as much as possible to train each man to tell others in the group directly what he thought about an issue. At the same time, I intervened directly in their process by passing on information and opinions if I felt this would aid the working situation.

A simple yet critical event will illustrate what I mean. Two members, Pete and Joe, did not always communicate freely with each other, partly because they felt some rivalry. Pete had completed a study and written a report which was to be discussed by the whole group. Three days before the report was due, I visited the company and stopped in at Pete's office to discuss the report with him and ask how things were going. He said they were fine, but frankly he was puzzled about why Joe hadn't come to him to look at some of the back-up data pertaining to Joe's function. Pete felt this was just another bit of evidence that Joe did not really respect Pete very much.

An hour or so later I was working with Joe, and raised the issue of the report. Joe and his staff were very busy preparing for the meeting but nothing was said about looking at the back-up data. When I asked why they had not done anything about the data, Joe said that he was sure it was private and would not be released by Pete. Joe wanted badly to see it, but felt sure that Pete had deliberately not offered it. I decided there was no harm in intervening at this point by reporting to Joe how Pete was feeling. Joe expressed considerable surprise; and later in the day, he went to Pete, who gave him a warm welcome and turned over to him three volumes of the data which Joe had been wanting to see and which Pete had wanted very much to share with him. I had to judge carefully whether I would hurt *either* Pete or Joe by revealing Pete's feelings. In this case I decided the potential gains outweighed the risks.

Getting back to setting the proper expectations on the part of the company, I have to make it very plain that I will not function as an expert resource on human-relations problems, but that I will try to help the group solve those problems by providing alternatives and by helping them to think through the consequences of various alternatives. I also need to stress my expectation that I will gather data primarily by observing people in action, not by interviewing and other survey methods (though these methods would be used whenever appropriate). Finally, I have to point out that I will not be very active, but will comment on what is happening or give feedback on observations only as I feel it will be helpful to the group.

The fact that I will be relatively inactive is often a problem for the group because of their expectation that once they have hired a consultant they are entitled to sit back and just listen to him tell them things. To have the consultant then spend hours sitting in the group and saying very little not only violates this expectation but also creates some anxiety about what he is observing. The more I can reassure the group early in the game that I am not gathering personal data of a potentially damaging nature, the smoother the subsequent observations will go.

In summary, part of the early exploration with the contact client and any associates whom he involves is intended to establish the formal and psychological contract which will govern the consultation. As I have indicated, I feel there should be no formal contract beyond an agreement on a *per diem* fee and a potential number of days to be devoted to working with the client system. Each party should be free to terminate or change the level of involvement at any time. At the psychological contract level, it is important to get out into the open as many misconceptions as possible, and to try to be as clear as possible about my own style of work, aims, methods, and so on.

A Final and Crucial Point. I reassure the client as much as possible that I will stay within the boundaries of the work projects which the group has set, and that I will not go into interpersonal areas or group processes unless the group first agrees to such exploration. The process consultant should not immediately become involved in discussing interpersonal processes with his client. Indeed, the client may be quite fearful of such discussions and be unwilling to proceed if he feels that he will inevitably find himself in a "T-group." Even though I observe such processes, my early interventions tend to stay very much at the level of how the group gets its formal work done, sets its agenda, and the like. Hence, my initial working agreement with the client is only to observe him and his group at work in order to identify potential areas of greater effectiveness and/or areas where effectiveness seems to be undermined.

I also reassure the client that I will not get into the specific content of what the group is talking about, but will focus primarily on *process issues.* This ground rule is negotiable at the initiative of either the group or the consultant.

10
SELECTING A SETTING AND A METHOD OF WORK

The final phase of the exploratory meeting or subsequent meetings involves the selection of a setting in which to work; the specification of a time schedule and a method of work; and preliminary statements about goals to be achieved in the particular setting chosen. These decisions are crucial because, by implication, they define the immediate client system to which the consultant will relate himself. I use a number of general criteria for making such decisions.

THE SETTING

1. *The Choice of What and When to Observe Should Be Worked Out Collaboratively with the Client.* The process consultant must avoid the image of a psychologist wandering around the plant making observations about anything that strikes him as needing attention. Instead, the consultant should engage in a focused process of observation and feedback where both participant and observer have agreed to inquire into the interpersonal process for the sake of improving it.

If the consultant feels the locus of observation should shift, he must involve the people who work in this new locus and establish a similar contract with them. Since the participants are themselves the targets of the process interventions, it is essential that they be involved in the decision to try to learn. Without this kind of psychological contract there is at best no readiness to hear what the consultant might have to say, and, at worst, real resentment at being observed by an outsider.

2. *The Setting Chosen Should Be as Near the Top of the Organization or Client System as Possible.* The reasons for beginning observations at the highest possible level are two-fold: first, the higher the level, the more likely it is that basic norms, values, and goals can be observed in operation. It is the higher levels that set the tone of the organization and ultimately determine the criteria for effective organizational functioning. If the consultant does not expose himself to these levels, he cannot determine what these ultimate norms, goals, and criteria are, and if he does not become acquainted with them, he is abdicating his own ethical responsibility. Only if the consultant can personally accept the norms, goals, and criteria of the organization can he justify helping the organization to achieve them. If the consultant feels that the organization's goals are unethical, immoral, or personally unacceptable for some other reason, he can choose to attempt to change them or terminate the relationship, but this choice should be made. The consultant should not operate in ignorance of what the established authority in the organization is trying to do.

Second, the higher the level, the greater the payoff on any changes in process which are achieved. In other words, if the consultant can help the president to learn more about organizational process and to change his behavior accordingly, this change in turn is a force on his immediate subordinates which sets a chain of influence into motion. The more general way to put this point is to say that the consultant should seek that setting or group of people which he considers to be *potentially most influential* on the rest of the organization. Usually this turns out to be the top executive group.

3. *The Setting Chosen Should Be One in Which It Is Easy to Observe Interpersonal and Group Processes.* Often this turns out to be a weekly or monthly staff meeting, or some regularly scheduled activity in which two or more of the members of the key group being observed transact business together. It is important to observe processes among the members, not just between individual members and the process consultant. For this reason, a survey or interview methodology is only a stopgap measure. Ultimately, the consultant must have access to a situation where the organization's members are dealing with each other in their usual fashion.

4. *The Setting Chosen Should Be One in Which Real Work Is Going On.* The consultant should avoid the situation where a group initially agrees to

meet with him only to discuss their interpersonal relations. Such a meeting would be appropriate after a relationship had developed between the group and the consultant but would be premature before. The group cannot as yet trust the consultant enough to really have an open discussion of interpersonal relations, and the consultant does not yet have enough observational data to be able to help the group in such a discussion. Regular committee or work-group meetings are ideal, on the other hand, because the consultant not only sees the organization members in a more natural role, but learns what sort of work the members are concerned about. At later intervention stages, it is much easier to link observations to real work behavior, and it is much more likely that real changes will occur in members if they can relate process observations to work events.

METHOD OF WORK

1. *The Method of Work Chosen Should Be As Congruent As Possible with the Values Underlying Process Consultation.* Thus observation, informal interviewing, and group discussions would be congruent with:

1. the idea that the consultant does not already have pat answers or standard "expert" solutions, and

2. the idea that the consultant should be maximally available for questioning and two-way communication.

If the consultant uses methods like questionnaires or surveys, he himself remains an unknown quantity to the respondent. As long as he remains unknown, the respondent cannot really trust him, and hence cannot really answer questions completely honestly. The method of work chosen, therefore, should make the consultant maximally visible and maximally available for interaction.

Often I choose to start a consultation project with some interviewing, but the purpose of the interview is not so much to gather data as to establish a relationship with each of the people who will later be observed. The interview is designed to *reveal myself* as much as it is designed to *learn something about the other person.* I will consider the use of questionnaires only after I am well enough known by the organization to be reasonably sure that people would trust me enough to give direct and frank answers to questions.

In the Apex Company, the exploratory meeting led to the decision to attend one of the regular meetings of the executive committee. At this time I was to meet the president and the other key executives to discuss further what could and should be done. At this meeting, I found a lively interest in the idea of having an outsider help the group and the organization to become more effective. I also found that the group was willing to enter an open-ended relationship. I explained as much as I could my philosophy of process consultation and suggested that a good way of getting further acquainted would be to set up a series of individual interviews with each member of the group. At the same time, I suggested that I sit in on the weekly half-day meetings of the executive committee. The interviews then would occur after several of these meetings.

At the initial meeting of the group, I was able to observe a number of key events. For example, the president, Alex, was very informal but very powerful. I got the impression initially (and confirmed it subsequently) that the relationships of all the group members to the president would be the key issue, with relationships to each other being relatively less important. I also got the impression that Alex was a very confident individual who would tolerate my presence only as long as he saw some value in it; he would have little difficulty in confronting me and terminating the relationship if my presence ceased to have value.

It was also impressive, and turned out to be indicative of a managerial style, that Alex did not feel the need to see me alone. He was satisfied from the outset to deal with me inside the group. Near the end of the initial meeting, I requested a private talk with him to satisfy myself that we understood the psychological contract we were entering into. He was surprisingly uncomfortable in this one-to-one relationship, had little that he wished to impart to me, and did not show much interest in my view of the relationship. I wanted the private conversation in order to test his reaction to taking some personal feedback on his own behavior as the consultation progressed. He said he would welcome this and indicated little or no concern over it. As I was to learn later, this reflected a very strong sense of his own power and identity. He felt he knew himself very well and was not a bit threatened by feedback.

In the Boyd Company, the consultation started in essentially the same manner. At the exploratory meeting with the president, Bill, I inquired whether there was some regular meeting which he held with his immediate subordinates. There was such a group which met weekly and it was agreed that I would sit in on it. Bill explained to the group that he had asked me to sit in to help the group function more effectively and then asked me to explain how I saw my own role. I described process consultation and the kinds of things I would be looking for; stated that I would not be very active, but preferred the group just to work along as it normally would; and that I would make comments as I saw opportunities to be helpful. It was decided that after a few meetings I would interview each member of the seven-man group individually.

The climate of the Boyd group was much more formal; there was less group participation, more reliance on Bill to run the meeting, and more ambiguity about the feelings of the members for each other.

In the Central Company the pattern was entirely different, since they were geographically removed and I had contracted to spend only one week with them at a time several months hence. The person coordinating my program was quite knowledgeable about the possible uses he could make of a process consultant and he had, as I indicated before, consulted with a colleague of mine to determine how best to use me. They decided that a workshop devoted to helping line managers improve their diagnoses and action plans for change programs which they wanted to implement was an appropriate workship goal. Once this had been decided by correspondence, I worked with my colleague on designing the program of the week. We corresponded further about this design, made some modifications, and then agreed not to freeze the plan until I was actually on the premises the evening before the workshop. We had, however, made the key decision to invite only managers who had an interest in changing some aspect of their immediate work situation, and to have each manager come with a member of the personnel staff reporting to him, so that *teams* would be looking at the change problems.

When I arrived at the Central Company site some months later, I met with my "inside" consultant contact, his boss (who was personnel director), and one or two other personnel people who were interested in the program. We reviewed the goals and schedule of the week, decided to remain flexible until we could find out more from the participants about their change goals, and agreed that the inside consultant would work with me in implementing the program. The setting for the program was the training center of the company. All the teams (eighteen men altogether), were to meet daily at the training center for the actual workshop.

In the case of Delta, the pattern was almost identical to Apex and Boyd. The head of the division with whom I had the exploratory lunch (Dave) decided that he wanted to build his group of immediate subordinates into an effective team so that they could manage what he saw as a difficult phase involving the rapid growth of the division. He held weekly staff meetings and invited me to sit in on these regularly. After several meetings I planned, as in the other cases, to interview each member of the seven-man group individually.

To illustrate a different kind of setting and work method I would like to refer to the Fairview Company. Some members of the training department had become exposed to sensitivity training several years back, had introduced it into their middle- and senior-manager development programs, and had gained a good deal of sophistication in analyzing organizational process. It became clear to a number of them that one of the major difficulties of the organization was conflict between the central headquarters and the various field units—conflicts over how much decentralization of decision-making authority there should be, conflicts concerning how much the system actually reflected earlier agreements to decentralize, and conflicts over lines of authority.

The organization had strong functional directors in the headquarters organization. As they developed financial and marketing programs they tended to bypass the formal line organization through the executive vice-president and the regional managers, dealing instead with the financial and marketing people in the field directly.

The central training group knew that there was an annual meeting of all the key executives including headquarters and field people, some fifteen in all. They consulted me about the possibility of organizing one of these meetings in such a way as to enable the entire group to work on the organizational problem. The training group was not sure how the president or vice-president would respond to the idea, since there was no prior history of exposure of the group to an outside consultant. However, a number of the regional managers had attended T-groups and learned something about the potential of bringing in a "behaviorally-oriented consultant." They felt strongly that something like this meeting should be tried.

A core group, consisting of the training director, two of his key staff people, and one enthusiastic regional manager, met with me for one day to plan further strategy. We decided that in order for such a program to work, it was necessary that some substantial number of the people who would eventually be at the meeting would also have to become involved in the planning and design of the meeting. This step was a crucial one, and rests squarely on the kind of theory which underlies process consultation. A group was formed consisting of equal numbers of headquarters and regional managers. The mission of this group was to meet for two days to plan the total meeting. The plan developed by the group was then to be presented for approval to the president and vice-president.

My role as a process consultant was critical at two stages in this enterprise. First, during the two-day meeting of the planning group, I had to steer them *away* from a traditional format in which I would make presentations about headquarters/field type problems for them to discuss. Secondly, I had to take responsibility for the success of the meeting format finally chosen and find a role for myself which would make this format work.

The plan which emerged from the two days of planning had the following elements:

1. The three day meeting would be billed as an exploration of organizational problems at the top of the organization, toward the end of improving organizational relationships;

2. The meeting would be chaired by me rather than the president of the company;

3. The agenda for the meeting would be developed by a procedure used by Richard Beckhard:

   Each member of the fifteen-man group would be asked to write me a letter at my home outlining what he saw to be the major organizational problems facing the group. It was then my job to put together the information from the fifteen letters into major themes and issues. These themes and issues were to be presented by me to the total group at our first session and would constitute the agenda for the three days.

The first purpose in having such letters written was to provide each person the opportunity to be completely frank without having to expose himself to the possible wrath of the boss or other members of the group. Secondly, it provided an opportunity to gather data from all the members before the meeting began. Third, it involved each member in helping to set the agenda, a considerable departure from previous meetings where the agenda had been set by the vice-president. It could be expected, therefore, that all the members would feel more involved in the meeting from the outset.

The letter-writing had two problems connected with it. It seemed a little bit gimmicky, and it was difficult to know how someone would react who had not as yet met me. Would he write a frank letter to a strange professor about rather critical organizational issues? We decided that we would have to run the risk of getting no response or poor response, but that we could minimize the risk by having the members of the planning group talk to others whom they knew and make a personal appeal to write a frank letter.

The procedure was agreed upon, was presented to the president and vice-president and received enthusiastic approval, and thus became the plan for the meeting. I pointed out that the president and vice-president would have to be careful in how they managed their own role. If they reverted too quickly to their power position and abandoned the role of helping to diagnose organizational problems, the group would retreat into silence and the problems would remain unsolved. I felt that both men understood the risks, were willing to take them, and had the kind of personality which would make them accept this somewhat strange meeting format.

Having agreed to go ahead, it was then decided that the vice-president would send out the letter explaining the meeting format and inviting the diagnostic letters. Members of the planning group were to follow up in the districts to ensure that everyone understood the plan and the fact that the plan had come from organization members themselves, even though I had suggested many of the separate elements.

This rather lengthy procedure was essential to obtain the involvement of the members in a process-oriented meeting. Even though the ideas came from the training department and from me, it clearly became a concept which appealed to regional and headquarters managers. Had they not become committed, it would not have been possible to hold such a meeting at all.

In summary, the choice of a setting and a method of work is highly variable. It is important that both the setting and working procedure be jointly decided between the contact client group and the consultant. Whatever decisions are made should be congruent with the general assumptions underlying P-C so that whatever changes result can be self-perpetuating.

11
GATHERING DATA

We will next discuss data-gathering as a separate stage, but I must emphasize most strongly the point that data-gathering and intervention occur simultaneously throughout the entire consultative process. Every decision to observe something, or to ask a question, or to meet with someone constitutes an intervention into the ongoing organizational process. The consultant cannot, therefore, avoid or escape taking the responsibility for the kind of data-gathering method he uses. If the method is not congruent with his overall values, and if it does not meet the standards for an acceptable intervention, it should not be used.

The point is worth belaboring because all of the traditional consultation models, as well as the models of how to do research on organizations, make the glib assumption that one gathers data prior to intervening; that one observes, interviews, and surveys, *then* makes a diagnosis, and *then* suggests interventions or remedial steps.

From the point of view of P-C this is an inaccurate and dangerous assumption. It is inaccurate because one can clearly demonstrate that the process of being studied influences the parties being studied. If I interview someone about his organization, the very questions I ask give the respondent ideas he never had before. The very process of formulating his own answers gives him points of view which he may never have thought of before. The assumption is also dangerous because the various respondents who have been interviewed, surveyed, or studied may, by virtue of this common experience, band together and decide on their own what kind of action they would like to see. While the researcher-consultant is off analyzing his data, the respondents are busy changing the organization or generating demands which their boss may be quite unprepared for.

What then is the correct assumption, and what are its implications? The correct assumption is that *every act on the part of the process consultant constitutes an intervention,* even the initial act of deciding to work with the organization. The very fact of having asked for help and having had someone accept some responsibility for helping, changes the perceptions and attitudes of some members of the organization. The process consultant cannot ignore these changes. He must anticipate them and learn to make them work toward the ultimate goals defined.

The main implication of this latter assumption is that the process consultant must think through everything he does in terms of its probable impact on the organization. He must assume that all of his behavior is an intervention of one sort or another. Finally, he must use data-gathering methods which, at the same time, will constitute valid and useful interventions.

METHODS OF DATA GATHERING

Basically the consultant has only three different methods by which he can gather data:

1) direct observation;
2) individual or group interviews;
3) questionnaires or some other survey instrument to be filled out.

I have already indicated that the third method is too impersonal and too much at variance with P-C assumptions to be useful in the early stages of a P-C project. It may become useful if the number of people to be surveyed is rather large and if the managers with whom the consultant is working fully understand the implications involved in taking a survey.

For early data-gathering the choice is then reduced to observation and/or interview. In my own experience I have found that a combination of these techniques is optimal. I need a certain amount of observation in order to know what kinds of issues should be brought up in interviews, but I need some preliminary interviews in order to know whom and what to observe.

These criteria usually lead to a top-down kind of strategy. I start with the data provided by the contact client. The exploratory meeting is usually an opportunity to gather data in a group-interview setting. As the cases above have shown, the next step is often an interview of one or more of the *senior* people who will be involved in the project. Their consent must be obtained to do any observation of them in interaction with their group. Regular group members are usually interviewed only after one or two meetings during which I have observed what kinds of issues are being discussed and what kinds of problems exist within the group.

Once a relationship has been formed with some key group in the organization, new projects develop which involve new settings, but the *methods* of gathering data in the new settings are essentially the same. For example, one of the managers of the original group may feel that he would like to know how the members of his own staff group feel about the organization and the work setting. He and I may then plan a series of interviews of his subordinates, leading to a series of feedback meetings. This procedure will not be initiated, however, until the manager has obtained the support and consent of his subordinates and until they too feel that I can be trusted. If it is not convenient for me to meet all of them and/or observe their meetings, a relatively greater burden falls on the manager to persuade his subordinates to participate; but the project cannot proceed until the subordinates genuinely agree.

In this connection, an important criterion for extending a data-gathering method is that the manager who would like to use it should himself have participated in an earlier project. If the manager has been interviewed by me and has heard what kind of feedback I give after a series of interviews, he is in a much better position to decide whether or not such a technique would be useful in his group, and is better equipped to explain to his subordinates what the procedure will be like.

No data-gathering method is right or wrong in the abstract. Whether or not it is appropriate and useful can be judged only from earlier observations and interviews. In a way the entire P-C project must always be viewed as an unfolding series of events where subsequent events can only be predicted from earlier events. The project should be planned in a general way, but the issues that come up in groups are hard to predict, and some of the most important ones are those for which the least planning was done.

What should be the content of interviews or surveys? I have already discussed at length the kinds of thing the consultant looks for when he observes a group in action. Now, what does he look for when he is interviewing and/or what kinds of questions does he build into a questionnaire? The answer is that it depends very much on the nature of the problem which is initially presented to the consultant and on his early observations.

For example, in the Apex Company, part of the initial mandate was to help the group to *relate to the president*. In the interviews which I conducted with group members, I concentrated quite heavily on what kinds of things went well in the relationship; what kinds of things went poorly; how relationship problems with the president were related to job performance; in what way the group members would like to see the relationship change, and so on. I did not have a formal interview schedule, but rather, held an informal discussion with each member around issues of the sort I have just mentioned.

In contrast, when I began to interview group members in the Boyd and Central Companies, I concentrated much more on what kind of job each member had, with whom he had to work in the performance of that job, what kinds of problems existed in any of these relationships, what organizational factors aided or hindered effective job performance, what the company climate was like, and so on.

In the case of the Delta Company, I gathered no data until the evening before the workshop, and subsequently within the workshop itself. In the Fairview Company, on the other hand, I gathered written data by means of the letters. In this case, each respondent was invited to put down whatever he saw as problems existing in the relationships between the headquarters organization and the various regional centers.

The common theme in all of these data-gathering approaches is a concern with organizational relationships and perceptions of organizational processes. The specific questions vary, but the general area is the same. The other common thread is a concern with organizational effectiveness. I always attempt to determine what kinds of things are helping to make the person, group, or unit more effective, and what kinds of things are undermining or hindering effectiveness. My assumption would be that both sets of factors are always present in any organization.

Having identified the kinds of content areas which I explore in interviews, I would like to close the loop to the earlier discussion of the kind of interventions I make when I interview somebody. For example, in the interview itself, my own method of asking questions and the content of what I ask will project a certain image of me. If I want to establish a collaborative, helping relationship with the person being interviewed, I must behave in a manner congruent with such a relationship. This means I cannot play the role of the psychologist who asks obscure questions upon which I then will place "secret" interpretations. My questions have to be understandable, relevant, meaningful, and open. The respondent should be able to interpret his own answers. There should be no trick questions, hidden meanings, obscure interpretations, or the like.

The content of the questions should be self-evidently relevant. If I am concerned about improving organizational effectiveness, then I should ask about it. If I am concerned with improvement, I should ask about those things that are going well, in addition to those which are going poorly.

The questions can push the respondent into areas he might not ordinarily think to mention, provided they are relevant and provided the consultant senses a willingness on the part of the respondent to enter into those areas. For example, in all of the cases mentioned, I asked quite probing questions about how the decision was made to use a consultant, the attitudes expressed by members toward my coming in, what they thought are my particular qualifications for the job, where there might be tension over having a consultant in, and so on. As I mentioned earlier, if the contact client is unwilling to deal with these areas openly in the early discussions, I am likely to be cautious about becoming involved. Once I am working within the organization, unwillingness to deal with areas such as these would be interpreted by me as caution on the respondent's part, and it would be up to me to try to determine what the reasons for the caution were.

The kind of question one asks also puts new ideas into the head of the respondent. For example, I often ask what kind of career planning a person has engaged in with others in the organization. The answer often is "none," but a secondary answer which comes up later in the interview is often "I wonder why no one has sat down with me to talk about my career," or "maybe I should go have a talk with my boss about my future in the company." If I ask a person to describe the network of others with whom he must deal in order to get his job done, he often realizes for the first time what this network is like and why he has problems of keeping up with his job. In other words, the interview can be a powerful tool of influence and education, and the process consultant must consider when and how to use it for influence purposes.

In summary, there are basically three kinds of data-gathering methods: observation, interview, and questionnaire. Because any one of the methods is some kind of intervention into organizational process, the consultant must choose a method which will be most congruent with the values underlying P-C and with the general goals of the P-C project. The way he gathers data and the kinds of question he asks gives the consultant an opportunity to intervene constructively. In the next section, we will take a closer look at intervention to explore more fully the options available to the consultant.

12
INTERVENTION

As I indicated in the chapter on data gathering, one cannot completely separate the stages of data-gathering and intervention. Both occur simultaneously: how one gathers data constitutes an intervention, and the kind of intervention one chooses will reveal new data derived from the reaction to the intervention. The separation of these two processes is, therefore, basically a matter of point of view or frame of reference. In this chapter I will focus on specific attempts to *change* organizational process by deliberate actions on the part of the consultant.

The interventions which a process consultant might make cannot be rigidly classified, but a broad categorization can be suggested:

1. *Agenda-setting interventions:*
   a) Questions which direct attention to interpersonal issues
   b) Process-analysis periods
   c) Agenda review and testing procedures
   d) Meetings devoted to interpersonal process
   e) Conceptual inputs on interpersonal-process topics

2. *Feedback of observations or other data:*
   a) Feedback to groups during process analysis or regular work time
   b) Feedback to individuals after meetings or after data-gathering

3. *Coaching or counseling of individuals or groups*

4. *Structural suggestions:*

    a)   Pertaining to group membership

    b)   Pertaining to communication or interaction patterns

    c)   Pertaining to allocation of work, assignment of responsibility, and lines of authority

The list is arranged in terms of a descending likelihood of use of the particular intervention. In other words, the kind of intervention I am most likely to make pertains to the group's agenda; the kind I am least likely to make is a structural suggestion. Actual solutions to management problems are not even listed because they would not be considered valid interventions in a P-C model. If I permitted myself to become interested in a particular management problem in sales, marketing, or production, I would be switching roles from that of process consultant to that of expert resource. Once I have become an expert resource, I find I lose my effectiveness as a process consultant.

AGENDA-SETTING INTERVENTIONS

The basic purpose of this type of intervention is to make the group sensitive to its own internal processes, and to generate on the part of the group some interest in analyzing these processes. In the early stages of a project, I often find myself suggesting to a group that they should allocate fifteen minutes or so at the end of their meeting to review the meeting. I may suggest some dimensions such as how involved they felt, how clear communications were, how well member resources were used, and so on. If the group is willing, I have them fill in a post-meeting reaction form (see pp. 42-43) and tabulate their own data for further discussion.

    If the group agrees to some period of time for process analysis, no matter how short, I can further stimulate their interest by asking them questions which direct the group's attention to process issues such as those discussed in Part 1 of this book. In addition, I will usually have observed particular events which have been important during the meeting.

    For example, in a number of meetings I have observed the chairman making decisions hastily and without full commitment from the group. My question during a process-review period then might be: "How did you all feel about the decision on topic X, how was the decision made, and how did you *feel* about how the decision was made?" I have to resist answering the question with my own feelings. First of all, my feelings might be irrelevant or untypical; and secondly, I want the group to learn to gather its own data and draw its own conclusions. If I am pressed, I will answer with my observation or my own feeling, but my preference would usually be to turn the question back to the group.

Out of process-analysis sessions there often arise two further issues, leading to further interventions. The group sometimes discovers that it has a variety of dissatisfactions with the manner in which it arrives at and processes its work agenda. I find myself at this point suggesting various ways by which the group can evaluate what to put on the agenda, how much time to allocate to each item, how to sort items in terms of importance or type of problem, and so on.

The other issue pertains to the matter of interpersonal process itself. The more interested the group becomes in its own workings, the more time it devotes to discussing this topic and the less time there is for its regular agenda. To deal with this dilemma I often suggest that process work could perhaps be done in depth by periodically allocating a whole meeting or some set block of time just to processes in the group.

Such meetings are often held away from the office at a motel or some other detached location, in order to permit the group to really work on group issues. I will not suggest this kind of meeting, however, until I believe the group is emotionally ready to handle a larger dose of process analysis. One of the frequent mistakes I have observed in colleagues' efforts to help organizations is an *initial* suggestion of holding a meeting to explore "relationships" and "interpersonal issues." Such a meeting should not be scheduled without first-hand knowledge that members want it and are ready to deal emotionally with whatever issues might come up.

The final subheading under agenda-setting interventions concerns the matter of presenting relevant elements of theory about individuals, groups, and the management process. I do not have a set pattern of what I will offer a group or when I will offer it, but some examples may make clear the use of this intervention.

In the Apex Company, I found that the treasurer consistently made the operating managers uncomfortable by presenting financial information in an unintentionally threatening way. He wanted to be helpful, and he felt everyone needed the information he had to offer, but it often had the appearance of an indictment of one of the other managers: his costs were too high, his inventory control had slipped, he was too high over budget, etc. Furthermore, this information was often revealed for the first time in the meeting, so that the operating manager concerned had no forewarning and no opportunity to find out why things had gone out of line. The result was often a fruitless argument about the validity of the figures, a great deal of defensiveness on the part of the operating manager, and irritation on the part of the president because the managers could not deal more effectively with the treasurer.

As I observed this process occurring repeatedly over several weeks, I decided that merely drawing attention to the pattern would not really solve the problem because everyone appeared to be operating with constructive intent. What the group needed was an alternative way to think about the use of financial control information. I therefore wrote a memo (see Appendix) on control systems and circulated it to the group. When this came up for discussion at a later meeting I was in a better position to make my observations about the group, since a clear alternative had been presented. My feeling was that I could not have successfully presented this theory orally because of the amount of heat the issue always generated, and because the group members were highly active individuals who would have wanted to discuss each point separately, making it difficult to get the whole message across.

In working with the Apex group I found the written "theory memo" a convenient and effective means of communication. With other groups I have found different patterns to be workable. For example, if the group gets away for a half-day of work on group process, I may insert a half-hour in the middle (or at the end) of the session to present whatever theory elements I consider to be relevant. The topics are usually not selected until I observe the particular "hang-ups" which exist in the group. I therefore have to be prepared to give, on short notice, an input on any of a variety of issues.

A final method of theory input is to make reprints of relevant articles available to the group at selected times. Often I know of some good piece of theory which pertains to what the group is working on. If I suggest that such an article be circulated, I also try to persuade the group to commit some of its agenda time to a discussion of the article.

The key criterion for the choice of theory input is that the theory must be relevant to what the group already senses is a problem. There is little to be gained by giving "important" theory if the group has no data of its own to link to the theory. On the other hand, once the group has confronted an issue in its own process, I am always amazed at how ready the members are to look at and learn from general theory.

Agenda-setting interventions may strike the reader as a rather low-key, low-potency kind of intervention. Yet it is surprising to me how often working groups arrive at an impasse on simple agenda-setting issues. In a way, their inability to select the right agenda for their meetings, and their inability to discuss the agenda in a constructive way, is symbolic of other difficulties which are harder to pinpoint. If the group can begin to work on its agenda, the door is often opened to other process discussions. Let me provide some case examples.

In the Apex company I sat in for several months on the weekly executive-committee meeting, which included the president and his key subordinates. I quickly became aware that the group was very loose in its manner of operation: people spoke when they felt like it, issues were explored fully, conflict was fairly openly confronted, and members felt free to contribute. This kind of climate seemed constructive, but it created a major difficulty for the group. No matter how few items were put on the agenda, the group was never able to finish its work. The list of backlog items grew longer and the frustration of group members intensified in proportion to this backlog. The group responded by trying to work harder. They scheduled more meetings and attempted to get more done at each meeting, but with little success. Remarks about the ineffectiveness of groups, too many meetings, and so on, became more and more frequent.

My diagnosis was that the group was overloaded. Their agenda was too large, they tried to process too many items at any given meeting, and the agenda was a mixture of operational and policy issues without recognition by the group that such items required different allocations of time. I suggested to the group that they seemed overloaded and should discuss how to develop their agenda for their meetings. The suggestion was adopted after a half-hour or so of sharing feelings. It was then decided, with my help, to sort the agenda items into several categories, and to devote some meetings entirely to operational issues while others would be exclusively policy meetings. The operations meetings would be run more tightly in order to process these items efficiently. The policy questions would be dealt with in depth.

Once the group had made this separation and realized that it could function differently at different meetings, it then decided to meet once a month for an entire day. During this day they would take up one or two large questions and explore them in depth. The group accepted my suggestion to hold such discussions away from the office in a pleasant, less hectic environment.

By rearranging the agenda, the group succeeded in rearranging its whole pattern of operations. This rearrangement also resulted in a redefinition of my role. The president decided that I should phase out my attendance at the operational meetings, but should plan to take a more active role in the monthly one-day meetings. He would set time aside for presentation of any theory I might wish to make, and for process analysis of the meetings. He had previously been reluctant to take time for process work in the earlier meeting pattern, but now welcomed it.

The full-day meetings changed the climate of the group dramatically. For one thing, it was easier to establish close informal relationships with other members during breaks and meals. Because there was enough time, people felt they could really work through their conflicts instead of having to leave them hanging. It was my impression that as acquaintance level rose, so did the level of trust in the group. Members began to feel free to share more personal reactions with each other. This sense of freedom made everyone more relaxed and readier to let down personal barriers and report accurate information. There was less need for defensive distortion or withholding.

After about one year the group decided quite spontaneously to try some direct confrontive feedback. We were at one of the typical monthly all-day meetings. The president announced that he thought each group member should tell the others what he felt to be the strengths and weaknesses of the several individuals. He asked me to help in designing a format for this discussion. I first asked the group members whether they did in fact want to attempt this type of confrontation. The response was sincerely positive, so we decided to go ahead.

The format I suggested was based upon my prior observation of group members. I had noticed that whenever anyone commented on anyone else, there was a strong tendency to answer back and to lock in on the first comment made. Hence, further feedback tended to be cut off. To deal with this problem I suggested that the group discuss one person at a time, and that a ground rule be established that the person being described was not to comment or respond until all the members had had a chance to give all of their feedback. This way he would be forced to continue to listen. The ground rule was accepted, and I was given the role of monitoring the group to ensure that the process operated as the group intended it to.

For the next several hours the group then went into a very detailed and searching analysis of each member's managerial and interpersonal style, including that of the president. I encouraged members to discuss both the positives and the negatives they saw in the other person. I also played a key role in forcing people to make their comments specific and concrete. I demanded examples, insisted on clarification, and generally asked the kind of question which I thought might be on the listener's mind as he tried to understand the feedback. I also added my own feedback on points I had observed in that member's behavior. At first it was not easy for the group either to give or receive feedback, but as the day wore on, the group learned to be more effective.

The total exercise of confrontation was considered highly successful, both at the time and some months later. It deepened relationships, exposed some chronic problems which now could be worked on, and gave each member much food for thought in terms of his own self-development. It should be noted that the group chose to do this spontaneously after many months of meetings organized around work topics. I am not sure they could have handled the feedback task effectively had they been urged to try sooner, even though I could see the need for this type of meeting some time before the initiative came from the group.

In the Apex case, my intervention tended to help the group move from chaotic meetings toward a differentiated, organized pattern. In the end, the group spent more time in meetings than before, but they minded it less because the meetings were more productive. The group has also learned how to manage its own agenda and how to guide its own processes.

In the Boyd Company a similar situation was present but the direction of learning was different. I found that the key Boyd group was strangling itself with formality and trivia. Agendas were long and detailed, meetings were highly formal, and members were responsible for reporting to the group on various operational issues on a carefully planned monthly schedule. If anyone tried to make comments on a report, he was quickly reminded that he knew less about the topic than the reporter. Consequently most of the talk during meetings was of a reporting, attack, or defense variety. Little open-ended problem-solving took place. Most members looked (and acted) passive and bored. When interviewed, they confirmed that they felt this way during meetings; yet, surprisingly, they tended to defend their meetings as necessary.

My own feeling was that the members were caught up in their own traditions. They had always run meetings this way; hence they felt that boredom and lack of involvement were the "normal" subjective feelings for participants in a meeting. Those who felt a little more frustrated and rebellious did not know what methods to follow for livelier, more productive meetings. Hence there were widespread feelings of apathy, resignation, and frustration.

I tried a whole series of interventions over a period of several months, most of them unsuccessful from my point of view. First, I asked the group to review its own agenda and share feelings about it. Some members revealed feelings of frustration but still staunchly defended the agenda pattern as necessary. Second, I tried to help the group to differentiate policy from operational decisions. It seemed to me that whenever they tried to discuss policy, operational problems would intervene and preempt a major portion of the time. I also felt that the group tended to hold too limited a concept of policy. The group verbally agreed with me, but failed to change its pattern of operation in any substantial way. Third, I tried being directly confrontive about the apathy and frustration which I saw in the members. The group accepted my confrontation like "good soldiers," defended itself a little bit, told me I had been very helpful, and then resumed its discussions in the old pattern.

A partial breakthrough came some months later. The president of the company had in the meantime attended a sensitivity-training lab and had come back with a somewhat greater enthusiasm for group-process work. He realized that the group could be more productive and recognized the need to make it so. We agreed to devote some time to discussion of what the group's agenda and pattern of operations should be. In the meantime, another event had taken place: the company had reorganized, putting responsibility for many of the day-to-day operational problems clearly on the shoulders of certain key individuals. In order to make the reorganization work, it was decided not to have as much group time devoted to reporting out and monitoring members' work areas.

When the group met to discuss its own future, some of the same depression which I had previously observed was still in evidence. After about twenty minutes of general discussion, I said in a rather exasperated tone that I never saw this group have any *fun*. What would it take to make people want to come to the meeting because the meeting would be *fun?* This comment released a burst of laughter, as if some kind of inner dam had burst. The group had really been operating on the assumption that work could *not* be fun, and was just silently taking its painful medicine.

Once this issue had been brought out into the open, members agreed that meetings could be more fun. In the subsequent discussion, members delineated several key requirements for better meetings: a climate of greater acceptance in the group which would permit members to share ideas, plans, and problems with each other, without feeling that they would be attacked by other members; more concentration on sharing information and problems, and less concentration on trying to make decisions in the group; and more effective use of group time by better agenda control.

The group spent an hour or more discussing how it might operate in the future, and, more importantly, agreed on the use of a process-analysis session at the end of each meeting, to review whether or not it was hitting its own targets. It was decided that one member of the group should be the process recorder and give feedback to the group at the end of the session. This decision was especially good since the members needed practice in observing group process. Shortly afterwards, my participation in the meetings was curtailed by other commitments, but recently I had an opportunity to discuss the group's progress with the president, and he feels that the meetings have improved, that the climate is more open, and that the process-observer role has been very helpful to the group in monitoring its own functioning.

This case illustrates for me the trial-and-error nature of intervention. I could not really have predicted which of my various efforts to loosen the group up would work. Indeed, if there had not been related changes such as the reorganization and the president's experience at the training laboratory, none of my efforts might have worked. Merely helping the group to identify its process does not automatically produce a change in that process, even if the group is quite frustrated and knows a change is needed.

FEEDBACK OF OBSERVATIONS OR OTHER DATA

a) *Feedback to Groups.* There are basically two types of circumstances which call for this type of intervention. Case 1 would be the situation where some group has agreed to a meeting in which interpersonal processes would be discussed, and has further agreed to have the consultant survey the members of the group for their individual reactions and feelings. The feedback of the survey results then serves as the opening agenda for the meeting. Case 2 is the situation where a group has already learned to discuss interpersonal process and has developed a need to supplement such discussion with more personal kinds of feedback. The meeting described in the previous section would be a good example of the latter type of situation.

It should be noted that in both types of situation there must be some readiness for active intervention or some consensus that feedback of observations or interview results would be a legitimate activity for the group to undertake. There is nothing more tempting for the process consultant than to leap in with his own observations as soon as he has picked up some data on an interesting issue. If the consultant is to maintain congruence with the P-C model, however, he must resist the temptation lest he put the group immediately on the defensive or undermine his own position by reporting something which does not make sense (or is unpalatable) to group members. The issue is not whether the observation is valid or not. The issue is whether the group is able and ready to understand and learn from the observation. Such ability and readiness must be built up before feedback can be useful.

The use of the first type of intervention—reporting back data gathered from individuals—is a very useful way to get the group oriented to what its process issues may be. The previously cited case of the Fairview Company illustrates the use of this device as a way to open a discussion. By having group members write to me about the major organizational issues which they perceived, it was possible for me to construct an agenda for the group which would maximize the probability that the group would confront issues which were of importance to the members. At the first meeting of the group I presented the major categories of issues which the letters had revealed, and tried to illustrate each issue by paraphrasing from one or more letters. The group was thus getting feedback, but the identity of the individual information source was protected.

I noticed during the three days of discussion that as the members became more comfortable with each other, they were increasingly able to make their own points and identify themselves openly with the various issues; they leaned less and less on me as the source of input. If the senior people in the group had reacted punitively to any of the issues brought up, the group would no doubt have avoided talking about those issues and there would have been less revelation of personal feelings. Furtunately the senior people were receptive, willing to listen to the issues, and able to work on them constructively.

In one of the divisions of the Apex Company, I followed a different procedure. After getting to know the top-management group through several group meetings, I suggested that it might be useful to interview and give feedback to the next level below the vice-president. There was some concern on the part of the senior group that there might be a morale problem at this level. Initially I was asked merely to do an interview survey and report back to the top group. I declined this approach for reasons already mentioned: gathering data to report to a higher group would violate P-C assumptions because it would not involve the sources of the data in analyzing their own process. I suggested instead that I conduct the interview with the ground rule that all my conclusions would first be reported back to the interviewee group, and that I would tell top management only those items which the group felt should be reported.[1]

---

1   This procedure was first brought to my attention as a method by Mr. Richard Beckhard.

The group would first have to sort the items and decide which things they could handle by themselves and which should be reported up the line of authority because they were under higher management control. The real value of the feedback should accrue to the group which initially provided the data; they should become involved in examining the issues they had brought up, and consider what they themselves might do about them.

The above-mentioned procedure was agreed upon by the top management. One vice-president sent a memorandum to all members who would be involved in the interview program, informing them of the procedure, his commitment to it, and his hope that they would participate. I then followed up with individual appointments with each person concerned. At this initial appointment I recounted the origin of the idea, assured the interviewee that his *individual* responses would be entirely confidential, told him that I would summarize the data by department, and told him that he would see the group report and discuss it before any feedback went to his boss or higher management.

In the interview I asked each person to describe his job, tell what he found to be the major pluses and minuses in the job, describe what relationships he had to other groups, and how he felt about a series of specific job factors such as challenge, autonomy, supervision, facilities, salary and benefits, and so on. I later summarized the interviews in a report in which I tried to highlight what I saw to be common problem areas.

All the respondents were then invited to a group meeting at which I passed out the summaries, and explained that the purpose of the meeting was to examine the data, deleting or elaborating where necessary, and to determine which problem areas might be worked on by the group itself. We then went over the summary item by item, permitting as much discussion as any given item warranted.

The group meeting had its greatest utility in exposing the interviewees, in a systematic way, to interpersonal and group issues. For many of them, what they had thought to be private gripes turned out to be organizational problems which they could do something about. The attitude "Let top management solve all our problems" tended to be replaced with a viewpoint which differentiated between intragroup problems, intergroup problems, and those which were higher management's responsibility. The interviewees not only gained more insight into organizational psychology, but also responded positively to being involved in the process of data-gathering itself. It symbolized to them top management's interest in them and concern for solving organizational problems. Reactions such as these are typical of other groups with whom I have tried the same approach.

Following the group meeting, the revised summary was then given to top management, in some cases individually; in others, in a group. My own preference is to give it first individually, to provide for maximum opportunity to explain all the points, and then to follow up with a group discussion of the implications of the data revealed in the interviews. Where the direct supervisor of the group is involved, I have often supplemented the group report with an individual report, which extracts all the comments made by interviewees concerning the strengths and weaknesses of the supervisor's style of management. These focused feedback items have usually proved of great value to the manager, but they should be provided only if the manager initially *asked for* this type of feedback.

In giving either individual or group feedback from the interview summary, my role is to ensure understanding of the data and to stimulate acceptance of it, so that remedial action of some sort can be effectively undertaken. Once the expectation has been built that top management will do something, there is great risk of lowering morale if the report is merely read, without being acted upon in some manner. Incidentally, it is the process consultant's job to ensure that top management *makes this commitment initially* and that high-level officials understand that when the interviews are completed there will be some demands for action. If management merely wants information (without willingness to do something about the information), the process consultant should not do the interviews in the first place. The danger is too great that management will not like what it hears and will suppress the whole effort; such a course will only lead to a deterioration of morale.

The results of interviews (or questionnaires) do not necessarily have to go beyond the group which is interested in them. One of the simplest and most helpful things a group can do to enhance its own functioning is to have the consultant interview the members individually and report back to the *group as a whole* a summary of its own members' feelings. It is a way of hauling crucial data out into the open without the risk of personal exposure of any individual if he feels the data collected about him are damaging or that the analysis of such data will result in conclusions that are overcritical of his performance.

b) *Feedback to Individuals.* This is an appropriate intervention when (1) some data have been gathered about the individual (by either interview or direct observation); and (2) the individual has indicated a readiness to hear such feedback. In the case where a number of subordinates have been interviewed, some of the comments they make will deal with their reactions to the boss's behavior. If the superior has agreed beforehand to listen to the others' reactions, it is quite appropriate for the consultant to describe the range of comments to him and to assist in interpreting the comments. If the consultant has been observing the boss in meetings, he can then add his own direct feedback and try to establish some relation between what he and the subordinates perceive. Sometimes there are no data from subordinates, only the consultant's observations. If the consultant feels that the manager is interested, and shows a readiness to listen and learn, it is entirely appropriate for the consultant to share these observations.

In order for feedback to be effective, the consultant must be able to ask the right questions, observe the relevant behavioral events, and give the feedback in a manner which will facilitate learning on the part of the recipient. The behavior asked about or observed must be relevant to the task performance of the group and to the goals of the total consultation project. The manner in which the feedback is given must reflect sensitivity to the blind spots or areas of defensiveness of the recipient. Feedback must be concrete, descriptive, verifiable, timely, and specific. The consultant must be prepared for defensiveness or too facile verbal acceptance, both of which imply a denial of the feedback. He must know how to impart potentially threatening information without demeaning the recipient. As I think back over my various consulting experiences, unquestionably the ones with the most disastrous results were those where I fed back "facts" without any concern for the feelings of the recipient. What then happened was that the facts were denied, and I was politely but firmly invited to terminate the relationship.

The giving of individual feedback can be illustrated from several cases. In the Apex Company I met with each of the vice-presidents whose groups had been interviewed and gave them a list of comments which had been made about their respective managerial styles. I knew each man well and felt that he would be able to accept the kinds of comments which were made. In each case we scheduled at least a one-hour session, so we could talk in detail about any items which were unclear and/or threatening.

These discussions usually become counseling sessions to help the individual overcome some of the negative effects which were implied in the feedback data. Since I knew that I would be having sessions such as these, I urged each interviewee to talk at length about the style of his boss and what he did or did not like about it. In cases where the boss was an effective manager, I found a tendency for subordinates to make only a few vague generalizations which I knew would be useless as helpful feedback. By probing for specific incidents or descriptions, it was possible to identify just what the boss did which subordinates liked or did not like.

In the Delta Company I was invited by the division manager to observe and comment on the regular staff meetings. In addition I held discussions periodically with the manager and was invited to comment on any aspects of his behavior which I had observed. He had formulated fairly specific goals for his meetings and was interested in the degree to which he was meeting those goals in his role as chairman. He asked for feedback from group members at the end of meetings, but also sought my observations.

In the workshops run for the Central Chemical Company, I concentrated primarily on the co-trainer, the member of the company who was working with me but wanted to learn how to run workshops like these on his own. After each session I would give him feedback on his participation in it, and, incidentally, solicit his feedback on my participation. As we learned to reciprocate with our observations, the feedback process became more meaningful to both of us.

As a rule I do not hesitate to ask members of the client organization to give me feedback on my own behavior as a consultant. Though they are usually reluctant to do so early in the relationship, I find that as we get to know each other, they become comfortable in telling me where I was effective or ineffective with them or with others. The ability to give me feedback in the two-man setting is, of course, an important skill which should transfer as an ability to be more open and direct with others in authority positions. The ability to give me feedback is also an important indicator of how well the initial problem of dependence on the consultant has been solved.

COACHING OR COUNSELING

The giving of feedback either to individuals or to groups almost invariably leads to coaching or counseling sessions. The manager may learn that he somehow fails to hear certain members of the group; that he does not give enough recognition for good performance; or that he is too unapproachable when the subordinate needs help. Inevitably his next question is "How can I change my behavior to achieve better results?" Similarly, a group may learn that its members see the meetings as dull or unfruitful; inevitably the members then ask "How can we make our meetings more interesting and productive?"

There are two cautions which the consultant must keep uppermost in his mind before answering the above questions:

1. Don't respond until you are sure that the group (or individual) has really understood the feedback and has been able to relate it to concrete observable behavior;

2. Don't respond until you are sure that the group member (or manager) has begun an active process of trying to solve the problem for himself.

If the consultant is not sure on point 1, he should continue to ask questions like: "What does that comment mean to you in terms of how you see yourself?" "Can you think of anything you do which might give people that impression?" Or "What do you think the giver of the comment was trying to get across to you?"

If the consultant is not sure on point 2, he can ask questions like: "Do you see anything in your own behavior which you could change?" "What might you do differently to create a different reaction?" Or "Do you really want to change your behavior?"

If the consultant gets responses like "I'm paying *you* to give me advice," he must reassess the state of the relationship and the readiness of the recipient of the feedback to work on the problem area. If the feedback has been sincerely sought and has been understood, it is most likely that the recipient will have ideas and will share these with the consultant. The consultant's role then becomes one of adding alternatives to those already brought up by the client, and helping the client to analyze the costs and benefits of the various alternatives which have been mentioned.

I do not wish in this short volume to go into the theory and practice of counseling; but I do wish to underline the basic congruence between theories of counseling and the theory of process consultation which I am trying to present here. In both cases it is essential to help the client improve his ability to observe and process data about himself, to help him accept and learn from feedback, and to help him become an active participant with the counselor/consultant in identifying and solving his own problems.

In all of the companies with which I have worked, there have arisen multiple opportunities to coach and counsel individuals or groups. There does not seem to be any particular pattern of timing to such sessions. Rather, I have had to be ready to sit down with people at such time as *they* were ready to examine some of their own behavior and consider alternatives. The major difference between being *only* a counselor and being a process consultant has been the fact that my data-gathering has given me information and perspectives which a counselor does not have. I have usually observed my client in action, and have heard what other people have said about him. This additional knowledge, when it is fed into the counseling sessions, enriches the choice of alternatives which can be considered, and opens up many of the problem areas to more concrete discussion.

For example, I have spent some hours with a manager who sees himself as a very progressive force in a rather conservative organization. My observations, and what others say about him, would suggest that he himself is rather conservative in his behavior. His *ideas* are progressive but his actual behavior tends to be stultifying to others. Our individual sessions are most productive when we can examine his self-image against what others say and what I have observed. As this manager learned to view his conservatism in action, he realized that he undermines some of his own progressive ideas. This realization has led to some marked changes of behavior and an increase in his effectiveness.

There is a close similarity between interventions which draw the group's attention to certain kinds of *process issues* and what I choose to call *counseling* (or *coaching*) types of interventions. One of the commonest opportunities to coach or counsel is to intervene when a particular event has occurred which is *typical of some problem* that the group is trying to overcome. At these times the consultant can be most effective by pointing out what has just occurred and inviting the group to examine the consequences. He is giving feedback at a timely moment in order to help the group to become more effective.

Let us look at some examples. In one company's executive-committee meetings I noticed that the group seemed to have low confidence in one of its members, the marketing manager. This lack of confidence was evident in the degree to which others ignored him, argued with him, and denigrated him outside the meetings. Every time this man attempted to explain any of his actions, decisions, or plans in the meetings, one of the more aggressive members would interrupt him and either answer for him or elaborate upon what he thought the marketing manager had said. The group seemed to expect this person to be weak and passive, and confirmed their expectation by preventing him from being anything else. I decided to intervene at the point where the behavior was most visible (i.e., just after the marketing manager had been ignored or interrupted on some issue), and to tell the group that I observed the pattern repeatedly. When I did this, the group expressed some interest in hearing whether the marketing manager did indeed feel cut off. He expressed some rather strong feelings confirming my observations. Once these feelings were known to the other members they began to listen more attentively to him. As they did so, they discovered that he had a lot to contribute and was anything but "weak" and "fuzzy-headed," as they had believed. Group members then began to trust his decisions more and became more comfortable in delegating authority to him.

In another group, the difficulty was related to the manner in which the boss of the group interacted with the members. The boss wanted the group members to be strong, self-reliant, confident decision-makers. He said this explicitly and his behavior implied it. I observed on repeated occasions that if any group member showed weakness in any form (not knowing what he wanted, having unclear plans, being unable to answer a critical question from another member), the head of the group would become very angry and belabor the person for many minutes on end. The more the head of the group pressed, the more silent, embarrassed, and unsure the target person became. In talking to such persons later, I often found that the only feeling they sensed in the head of the group was blind anger, and this made them so defensive that they could not hear what he really wanted of them. In this case I tried to interrupt the process in midstream and collect feelings both from the person being belabored and from other members of the group. In addition I gave direct feedback to the group head, both in front of the group and later privately, concerning the impact his behavior was having on me. This led to some analysis of the behavior and a gradual shifting away from communication of anger toward communication of disappointment, which in turn made it possible for the group to home in on the issue that was really bothering them.

STRUCTURAL SUGGESTIONS

As I indicated at the outset of this chapter, this kind of intervention is very rare, largely because it violates some of the basic assumptions of the process-consultation model. The consultant is rarely in a position to suggest how work should be allocated, or communication patterns altered, or committees organized. The most he can do is help the manager to assess the consequences of different alternatives, or suggest alternatives which have not been considered.

For example, in a company which had recently gone from a functional to a product-line organization, I noticed that communication among the functional people (e.g., in marketing and engineering), had been reduced very sharply. My intervention was designed to draw attention to the fact that any form of organization has both strengths and weaknesses. Hence the manager needs to make an effort to create *informal* structures to compensate for the weaknesses created by the formal structure. In this case, the company eventually adopted a committee structure which brought the functional specialists together on a regular basis and thus reduced the communication gap which had resulted from the reorganization.

The consultant must make it quite clear that he does not propose any particular solution as the best one. However frustrating it might be to the client, the process consultant must work to create a situation where the client's ability to *generate his own solutions* is enhanced. The consultant wants to increase problem-solving ability, not to solve any particular problem.

In my experience there has been only one class of exceptions to the above "rule." If the client wants to set up some meetings specifically for the purpose of working on organizational or interpersonal problems, or wants to design a data-gathering method, then the consultant indeed does have some relevant expertise which he should bring to bear. From his own experience he knows better than the client the pros and cons of interviews or questionnaires; he knows better what questions to ask, how to organize the data, and how to organize feedback meetings; he knows better the right sequence of events leading up to a good discussion of interpersonal process in a committee. In such matters, therefore, I am quite direct and positive in suggesting procedures, who should be involved in them, who should be told what, and how the whole project should be handled.

For example, recall that in the Apex Company the president decided at one of their all-day meetings to try to give feedback to all the members. He asked me to suggest a procedure for doing this. In this instance I was not at all reluctant to suggest, with as much force and logic as I could command, a particular procedure which I thought would work well. Similarly, when it was proposed to interview all the members of a department, I suggested exactly how this procedure should be set up; I explained that all the members had to be briefed by the department manager, that a group feedback meeting would have to be held, and so on.

I have not been at all hesitant in refusing to design a questionnaire study if I thought it was inappropriate, or to schedule a meeting on interpersonal process if I thought the group was not ready.

In conclusion, the process consultant should not withhold his expertise on matters of the learning process itself; but he should be very careful not to confuse being an expert on *how to help an organization to learn* with being an expert on the *actual management problems* which the organization is trying to solve. The same logic applies to the evaluation of individuals: I will under no circumstances evaluate an individual's ability to manage or solve work-related problems; but I will evaluate an individual's readiness to participate in an interview survey of his group or a feedback meeting. If I feel that his presence might undermine some other goals which the organization is trying to accomplish, I will seek to find a solution which will bypass this individual. These are often difficult judgments to make, but the process consultant cannot evade them if he defines the *overall health of the organization* as his basic target. However, he must always attempt to be fair both to the individual and the organization. If no course of action can be found without hurting either, then the whole project should probably be postponed.

I can give two further examples of structural interventions. In Company G, not previously referred to, I have worked for some time with a member of the corporate management-development group. I have functioned primarily as an adviser, counselor, and sounding-board on various programs being developed by the group. The organization does not have major aspirations in the organizational development direction, though there is a growing interest in this kind of activity. Sometime last year, the inside manager was requested to consider a training program for all of the key marketing people in the various divisions of the company. I was called in to help design this program and to function as a staff member in it. My responsibilities included the recruiting of another staff member, helping members of management formulate their hopes and needs for the program, and then helping to design the actual program. This required a shift in role from being a process consultant to being an expert resource on the design and execution of a management-training program.

In my relationship with Company G, I find myself making this switch from time to time. The role switching works because of the fact that I have worked with this client company for a number of years, and the client contact is himself comfortable in playing and adapting to different roles in the relationship. The primary contact also functions as a point of communication with other groups in the organization where process consultation is needed from time to time. For example, I have worked with a sales group in one of the divisions of the company on an interview-feedback project, in determining how the members of the operating sales force in one region were viewing their job, and in helping management to reassess the overall style of operation in the sales function.

The second example comes from Company B. My primary work in this organization has been to meet with the top-management group and to counsel individual members of the group. Last year I was asked by the personnel director to become involved in the annual manpower survey and to help the organization design a more coherent overall approach to management development. To accomplish this task I asked to be a part of the manpower committee. During the meetings I attempted to assess the needs of the organization and the kind of program which would meet these needs. In doing this I was beginning to shift toward being an expert resource and abandoning the P-C role.

It seemed to me, as I listened to the discussions, that the group would fall short of generating a clear concept of a program in the time it had allotted to itself; hence I intervened "structurally" and suggested a multicomponent program of self-development, systematic use of internal and external training, and a revision of policies of recruiting and utilizing people in the organization. All of the points were extrapolations of what members of the committee wanted to do, but I put it together into a total framework and made some effort to "sell" it to the group. The group adopted the program and made a proposal of it to other members of management and the board.

In looking back upon this intervention, I have wondered whether the structural nature of it was indeed warranted and whether my own goals were truly accomplished or not. There is some evidence that the program has been bought in principle and that everyone agrees to it intellectually, but there has been relatively little move to implement it. At least one possibility as to why it has not been more systematically implemented is that I went too far beyond the group with my intervention—somehow the group lost ownership of the program and hence felt no real commitment to implement it. If this hypothesis is correct, it illustrates nicely the fine line between process and expert consultation and the inherent dangers of structural interventions.

SUMMARY

I have tried to draw attention to the varieties of intervention which the process consultant uses. I hope it is clear to the reader that the essence of the process-consultation model is to continuously rediagnose and to act accordingly. Therefore, one cannot specify particular recipes for intervention or particular sequences which should be used in any given project. A sequence which may work in Company A may be all wrong in Company B. Instead, the consultant must be ready to intervene in a variety of ways as opportunities arise and as his judgment tells him certain actions are appropriate. He must be flexible enough to take advantage of opportunities based on his own judgments.

The kinds of intervention which were reviewed were:

1) agenda setting through questions, through process analysis periods, through meetings devoted to interpersonal and group process, and through theory inputs on various process issues;

2) various kinds of feedback sessions to individuals or groups, based either on observed data or data obtained in interviews;

3) coaching or counseling which occurs either in specific sessions devoted to that purpose or as part of an on-going interaction in a group; and

4) structural suggestions pertaining to process oriented meetings or other parts of the consultation project.

13
EVALUATION OF RESULTS AND DISENGAGEMENT

So far in this book we have examined in some detail the thinking and activities of a process consultant. We have not concentrated on the big picture: what kinds of outcome or result does the process consultant look for over a period of time, how does he measure these outcomes, and how does he decide at some point to reduce his involvement with the client system?

These questions will not be easy to answer because the goals of P-C cannot be stated in simple measurable terms. The ultimate goal of any organization-development effort is, of course, improved organizational performance. Those organization-development efforts which involve P-C attempt to achieve this effectiveness by changing some of the *values* of the organization and by increasing the *interpersonal skills* of key managers. Performance is, in turn, related to these value changes and increases of skill. In the short run, then, the process consultant looks for evidence that certain values are changing and that certain skills are increasing. Let us look at what these values and skills are.

VALUES AND SKILLS TO BE CHANGED
THROUGH PROCESS CONSULTATION

Values

The single most important value to be changed in any organization-development effort involving P-C concerns the relative attention given to task *vs.* human concerns. Most managers start with the value that the most important concerns of management are efficient task performance primarily, and human relations secondarily (or as time permits). The problem for the process consultant is to change this value—make the manager feel that human relations and the management of interpersonal and group events is at least as important as immediate task performance. The logic behind this value is that for the manager his task can only be accomplished through other people; hence effective interpersonal relations become a prime means to the end of efficient task performance. Organizations in the end are nothing more than networks of human relationships. If these networks do not function effectively there is nothing with which to perform the tasks to be accomplished.

A *second* value which has to be changed in any OD effort involving P-C concerns the relative attention given to the content of the work and the structure of the organization *vs.* the *process* by which work is done. Managers tend to focus much more on the content of decisions, interactions, and communications. They tend to devalue the importance of "personality," of "feelings," and of "how things are done," or they attempt to dodge such process-related issues by perpetual redesign of the structure of the organization. The process consultant faces the problem of showing managers that processes in the organization follow patterns which can be studied and understood, and which have important consequences for organizational performance. Most importantly, processes can be rationally changed and adapted to increase the effectiveness of performance. Therefore, one should attempt to improve the organization through a joint consideration of the structure and of the processes of the organization.

A *third* value concerns the relative attention given to *short-run output* vs. *long-run effectiveness.* Most managers feel that every hour of every day should be occupied with activities that have an immediate output. The process consultant knows from his experience that the diagnosis of interpersonal events often involves periods of slow and calm analysis which may at first appear to be a terrible waste of time. He must change the manager's value system, so that he becomes tolerant of such periods, in the realization that the time invested in building *effective interpersonal relations* leads to much quicker and more effective *ultimate task performance.*

A *fourth* value which the process consultant must inculcate is the acceptance of the need for *perpetual diagnosis* as an alternative to insistence on *generalizations and principles* by which to operate. It is my assumption that the rate of change in the environment (and, therefore, within organizations) will increase, and that this in turn will require an increase in the organization's ability to diagnose both the environment and itself. A principle may hold up for the next six months but may be invalid within a year. The manager must accept perpetual diagnosis of process as a way of life if he is to avoid obsolescence and organizational failure. Ideally, the manager would not merely accept this value grudgingly, but would discover that perpetual diagnosis can be fun and can lead to perpetually better day-to-day task performance. I am not advocating what so many managers seem to fear—that if they do too much diagnosis they will be unable to be decisive when an occasion demands it. I am advocating that decisions be made, within the time constraints imposed by the task requirements, but that they be made in terms of a *diagnosis,* however short, rather than a *policy* or *general principle* which may no longer have any validity.

In summary, the process consultant attempts to change the manager's attitudes and values in the direction of more concern for human problems, more concern for process issues, more concern for long-run effectiveness, and more concern for the diagnostic process itself as a way of achieving organizational adaptability. By implication, one major way in which to assess the results of a P-C effort is to gauge the degree to which these values have taken hold in key managers. Such an assessment cannot be made formally or through some kind of specific measuring tool. It must be made by the consultant through observation of the activities of managers in the organization, or by the managers themselves.

Skills

As I have been repeating endlessly throughout this volume, the most important skill to be imparted to the client is the ability to diagnose and work on his own problems in the interpersonal, group, and organizational area. Initially the process consultant has more knowledge and skill than the client. As the P-C effort progresses, he should be able to observe an increase in the knowledge and skill of the various managers who have been involved. One of the best indicators of the growth of such skills is the willingness of various groups or teams to tackle process-analysis periods or agenda-review periods by themselves. How willing are they to assign an observer role, and how skillful are they in picking out key group events, in sharing feelings, in reviewing group action?

It should be clear that a willingness to engage in activities which initially have been the consultant's reflects a change in values. Even if a given manager were able to engage in more self-diagnostic processes, he might resist such an activity if none of the values cited above had changed. On the other hand, willingness reflecting a value change is not enough if there has not been a corresponding development of skill.

The assessment of the skill of the client system in diagnosing and working on its own problems must, as in the case of values, be made by observations on the part of the consultant and/or by the client system itself. It is important that managers feel confident in solving their own problems, and solving them effectively. Even if the consultant doubts that the level of skill reached is sufficient, he must be prepared to back off if members of the client system themselves feel they are able to go ahead without his help.

In Case A, considerable value change and skill growth occurred over the course of the first year. During this time I spent a great deal of time in two major activities: (1) sitting in on various meetings of the top-management group; and (2) conducting interview and feedback surveys of various key groups, as managers decided they wanted such interviews done. In addition there were periods of individual counseling, usually resulting from data revealed in the interviews.

I have already given examples of the kinds of specific activities which occurred in the group meetings, interviews, and feedback sessions. It was clear that with increasing experience, the group was learning to tune in on its own internal processes (skill), was beginning to pay more attention to these and to give over more meeting time to analysis of interpersonal feelings and events (value change), and was able to manage its own agenda and do its diagnosis without my presence (skill). The group first discovered this from having to conduct some of its all-day meetings in my absence. Where such meetings used to be devoted entirely to work content, the group found that even in my absence they could discuss interpersonal process with profit. The members themselves described this change as one of "climate." The group felt more open and effective; members felt they could trust each other more; information was flowing more freely; less time was being wasted on oblique communications or political infighting.

During the second year, my involvement was considerably reduced, though I worked on some specific projects. The company had set up a committee to develop a management-development program. I was asked to sit in with this committee and help in the development of a program. After a number of meetings, it became clear to me that the kind of program the group needed was one in which the content was not too heavily predetermined. The problems of different managers were sufficiently different to require that a formula be found for discussing the whole range of problems. One of the reflections of the value change which had taken place in the managers was their recognition that they should be prime participants in any program which they might invent. If a program was not exciting or beneficial enough to warrant the committee's time, it could hardly be imposed on the rest of the organization.

We developed a model which involved a series of small-group meetings at each of which the group would set its own agenda. After every third meeting or so, a larger management group would be convened for a lecture and discussion period on some highly relevant topic. Once the first group (the committee plus others at the vice-president level) had completed six to eight meetings, each member of the original group would become the chairman for a group at the next lower level of the organization. These ten or so next-level groups would then meet for six to eight sessions around agenda items developed by themselves. In the meantime the lecture series would continue. After each series of meetings at a given organizational level, the model would be reassessed and either changed or continued at the next lower level with the previous members again becoming group chairmen.

My role in this whole enterprise was, first, to help the group to invent the idea; second, to meet with the original group as a facilitator of the group's efforts to become productive; third, to serve as a resource on topics to be covered and lecturers to be used in the lecture series; and fourth, to appear as an occasional lecturer in the lecture series or as a source of input at a small-group meeting. As this procedure took form, my involvement was gradually reduced, though I still meet with the original committee to review the overall concept.

In recent months I have met occasionally with individual members of the original group and with the group as a whole. My function during these meetings is to be a sounding-board, to contribute points of view which might not be represented among the members, and to help the group assess its own level of functioning. I have been able to provide the group with some perspective on its own growth as a group because I could more easily see changes in values and skills. It has also been possible for the group to enlist my help with specific interpersonal problems. A measure of the growth of the group has been its ability to decide when and how to use my help, and to make those decisions validly from my point of view in terms of where I felt I could constructively help.

In Company B, my participation was similar, but for a variety of reasons changes in the organization have occurred much more slowly. The top-management group has accepted many of the values at an intellectual level but has not really committed itself to trying to make them work. Some members of the group have worked much harder at this than others. At the level of skill development, the group has experimented with a variety of techniques, such as having a member of the group be an observer and then report back. These activities have had a noticeable (though not a great) impact. Part of the problem in this company is that they have had to fight a number of traditions which are, in varying degrees, out of line with the kinds of values I have espoused. They have also faced a number of crises which required immediate action and which eroded efforts to concentrate on increasing diagnostic and interpersonal skills.

In recent months I have continued to meet both with individuals and with the group as a whole. My activities involve counseling members of the group and keeping a gentle but firm pressure on members of the system to become more open, trusting, and, thereby, effective. Recently the group decided on its own to hold a two-day meeting at which some strong personal feelings were shared by members of the group. Though the experience was traumatic for one or two members, the feeling of most was that it had been constructive and they looked forward to more of the same at some later time. My role in the meantime is to help them to understand the emotional experience they have been through and show them how to turn it into a constructive experience.

In Company D, I found the key group to be from the start relatively high in its acceptance of organization-development values and in its level of skill. After a dozen or so meetings the group and I reviewed the project and decided that for the moment nothing more was needed. As problems developed, the group would resume contact with me. Some months later the group had to be expanded because the whole division which was involved was to be expanded. With the expansion came some potential new problems. Because the diagnostic skill of the group was already high, I was called in again to make some plans for a longer meeting at which some of the new problems would be explored in depth.

Process consultation is an emergent process and therefore it is difficult to put simple boundaries upon it. Similarly, it is difficult to give overall evaluations. One can look at gradual changes which occur in the culture of the client organization; one can look at the results of specific projects like an interview-feedback cycle; and one can assess the immediate impact of an intervention in a group. But one cannot measure specific indicators, however much this might be desirable. In the end, the outcome of a period of process consultation must be judged jointly by members of the client system and the consultant. Both must make a judgment of whether to continue the relationship and in what manner to continue it. If, in the judgment of either party, there should be a reduction of involvement, how is this process accomplished?

DISENGAGEMENT: REDUCING INVOLVEMENT WITH THE CLIENT SYSTEM

The process of disengagement has, in most of my experiences, been characterized by the following features:

1. reduced involvement is a mutually agreed upon decision rather than a unilateral decision by consultant or client;

2. involvement does not generally drop to zero but may continue at a very low level;

3. the door is always open from my point of view for further work with the client if the client desires it.

Let me comment upon each of these points, and give some examples.

1. *Joint Decisions.* In most of my consulting relationships there has come a time when either I felt that nothing more could be accomplished and/or some members of the client system felt the need to continue on their own. To facilitate a reduction of involvement, I usually check at intervals of several months to see whether the client feels that the pattern should remain as is or should be altered. In some cases where I have felt that a sufficient amount had been accomplished, I have found that the client did not feel the same way and wanted the relationship to continue on a day-a-week basis. In other cases, I have been confronted by the client, as in Company A, with the statement that my continued attendance in the operational group meetings was no longer desirable from his point of view. As the president put it, I was beginning to sound too much like a regular member to be of much use. I concurred in the decision and reduced my involvement to periodic all-day meetings of the group, though the initiative for inviting me remained entirely with the group. Had I not concurred, we would have negotiated until a mutually satisfactory

arrangement had been agreed upon. I have sometimes been in the situation of arguing that I remain fully involved even when the client wanted to reduce involvement, and in many cases I was able to obtain the client's concurrence.

The negotiation which surrounds a reduction of involvement is in fact a good opportunity for the consultant to diagnose the state of the client system. The kinds of arguments which are brought up in support of continuing (or terminating) provide a solid basis for determining how much value and skill change has occurred. The reader may feel that since the client is paying for services, he certainly has the right to make unilateral decisions about whether or not to continue these services. My point would be that if the consultation process has even partially achieved its goals, there should arise sufficient trust between consultant and client to enable both to make the decision on rational grounds. Here again, it is important that the consultant not be economically dependent upon any one client, or his own diagnostic ability may become biased by his need to continue to earn fees.

2. *Involvement Not Zero.* If the client and consultant agree on a reduced involvement, it is important that both should recognize that this does not necessarily mean a complete termination. In fact, a complete termination is not desirable because the diagnosis on which reduced involvement is based may not be accurate enough to warrant termination. A more desirable arrangement is to drop the level to perhaps a half-day every three or four weeks, or attendance only at certain kinds of special meetings, or an interview with key members of the client system once every two or three months. Through this mechanism it is possible for the client and the consultant to reassess periodically how things are going.

In Company B, there was a period where I felt that a plateau had been reached. At this point I suggested that I reduce my involvement to a half-day every other week, and even then only if specific individuals wanted to have some time to talk over problems with me. After a few months at this reduced level, a number of events made it more important than ever for the top management group to increase their level of effectiveness. The group decided to have more meetings and asked me to become reinvolved at an increased level. This decision was much easier to negotiate from a reduced involvement than it would have been from a situation where I had terminated the relationship completely.

In my relationship with Company F, there are long periods where I do not pay any visits, but it is understood that as problems or issues come up the client is free to call on me with the expectation that I will respond positively. The only problem with this kind of arrangement is that it makes it difficult for the consultant to plan his time. Obviously if several clients decide to increase their involvement all at the same time, it may be impossible for the consultant to respond. If this occurs, the consultant has to be open about his dilemma and determine from the various clients whether or not they can wait for a month or so. I have found from experience that I can carry about four clients at any given time, with two of them being more active (one half-day every week), while two others are "dormant" (an occasional visit every three weeks to a month).

3. *Reinvolvement Is Always Possible.* This point is closely related to the previous one, but I want to separate it to bring out a special aspect of the obligation of the process consultant. In any P- C consulting relationship with a client, I think the consultant should make it clear that the door is always open to further work once the relationship has begun. The reason for this obligation is that a good relationship with a consultant is difficult for a client to develop. Once both the consultant and the client have invested effort in building such a relationship it does not terminate psychologically even if there are prolonged periods of lack of contact. I have had the experience with a number of clients of not seeing them for many months and yet being able to tune in on the group very quickly once contact has been reestablished.

As a general rule it should be the client who reestablishes contact, but I would not advocate sticking to this rigidly. I have, after some period of no contact, called a client and asked if I could talk with him to find out what was going on. In several cases such a call was welcomed and served as the basis for some additional counseling or process observation. The consultant must be careful not to violate his role by selling himself back to the client. It must be an honest inquiry which can comfortably be turned down by the client should he desire to do so. I have been turned down often enough to know that there is nothing inherent in the situation to force an artificial contact. Rather, it sometimes helps a client who wanted help anyway to ask for it in a face-saving way.

14

PROCESS CONSULTATION IN PERSPECTIVE

As I look back over this book I realize that I have had several purposes in mind in writing it. First, I wanted to expound a model of the consultation process which, I believe, describes what the typical consultant does (or should do) in an organization-development effort. Many of the volumes in this series give an overview of organization development but do not give a detailed view of the consultant's day-to-day operation. Second, I wanted to try to explain as clearly as I could what has gone on between me as a consultant and a number of clients I have had over the years. I have found that some of my colleagues have entertained some remarkable misconceptions about what I did when I went off to visit a company. I want to clear away some of these misconceptions. Third, I want to contribute to the general theory of organizational consultation by illustrating clearly one style of working with an organization. In view of the increasing amount of research and consultation in complex organizations, it is important to know clearly what one is doing. I hope I have clarified some of the issues by laying out the concept of process consultation.

I should like to close this volume by making a few general comments about process consultation in relation to other kinds of activities, as a way of giving some perspective to this procedure. Process consultation, first of all, is a way of *studying* organizations. I believe very much in Lewin's dictum: "If you want to understand something, try to change it." Much of the consultant's satisfaction comes from the combination of exercising a diagnostic and intervention skill while being constantly exposed to organizational process from which he learns what goes on in organizations. This exposure has enriched and sharpened my teaching and research skills.

One of my colleagues asked me why I bothered to teach a very small number of managers elementary principles of psychology, when I could be writing research papers which would influence thousands. The first answer is that P-C is anything but the teaching of elementary psychology. For me it is a complex process of producing changes in the organization which are not achievable by any amount of good writing. The change process is one not merely of transmitting ideas, but of changing values and of teaching skills. I derive far more satisfaction from improving an organization's effectiveness than I would from teaching a few managers some psychology which they might not know how to apply anyway. The second answer is that research which is done on organizations by people who do not get close to organizational processes has, to me, a kind of unreal quality about it—unreal because in focusing on concepts which are so far removed from the immediate experiences of members of the organization, one does not know how to generalize from the results. On the other hand, the kind of diagnosis which occurs when one conducts a series of interviews or observes groups in action brings organizational phenomena to life. The systematic reporting out of such data is undoubtedly of high value.

The third, and, perhaps most important, answer is that my teaching would be sterile without the kind of "feel" one gets from close contact with organizations. I could, of course, periodically immerse myself completely, by taking a job in an organization. Apart from the fact that I would not like the dislocation involved, I am not sure that such a complete transition would be necessary to get the kind of feel I am talking about.

The process consultant often operates in industry in much the same way a general practitioner does in medicine; he is, in a sense, an *organizational internist*. The analogy holds if one thinks of the consultant as helping the organization to arrive at a diagnosis before deciding on some specialized treatment. The analogy breaks down, however, if one considers that the internist is the prime expert in the diagnosis. He runs tests, asks questions, pokes about, and then delivers a diagnosis and advice. The process consultant, in contrast, attempts to involve the organization in *self*-diagnosis and enables the organization to give itself sound advice.

A better analogy is to think of the process consultant as a sociotherapist or as a T-group trainer, for a system which varies in size and composition from time to time. The concepts of "diagnosis" and "helpful intervention" derive directly from the concept of laboratory training. The major difference between helping a group and consulting for an organization lies in the complexity of the task. To be an effective process consultant, the person needs diagnostic and intervention skills which are quite different from those used in a human-relations training group. The process consultant does not have the environmental supports of a laboratory; he cannot count on the intensive involvement that lab groups generate; he cannot even assume a commitment to learning comparable to that of the lab participant. Through his own interventions, from an ambiguous power base, and in the midst of on-going work, he must build involvement and commitment, and must gain acceptance for the importance of looking at process.

The sociotherapist model suggests itself if one considers that the consultant is primarily dedicated to helping the system help itself in terms of whatever pathology he may find there. Once an initial contract has been established, the consultant must be prepared to work with whatever he finds, and he must, like the individual therapist, be very careful not to suggest things to the patient which will be misunderstood, not to give advice which will be resisted, and not to fall into the trap of thinking he is an expert on that particular organization. All he is expert at is giving help. On the other hand, the sociotherapist model also has limitations in that it suggests pathology. In my experience it is the *healthy* organization that knows enough to expose itself to help to ensure its future health. Sick organizations tend to resist the kind of help which process consultation could perhaps offer them.

As a final thought, I would like once again to contrast P-C with more standard kinds of consultation models. The standard model is one in which the consultant gives expert advice on how to solve a particular problem which the organization has identified: how to improve production scheduling, how to determine costs, how to obtain marketing information, how to increase productivity, how to select and train certain kinds of personnel, etc. Even if initial work with the consultant leads to a redefinition of the problem, the consultant's task remains the same: help develop an expert solution.

The process model, in contrast, starts with the assumption that the organization knows how to solve its particular problems or knows how to get help in solving them, but that it often does not know how to *use its own resources effectively* either in initial problem solution or in implementation of solutions. The process model further assumes that inadequate use of internal resources or ineffective implementation result from process problems. By this I mean that people fail to communicate effectively with each other, or develop mistrust, or engage in destructive competition, or punish things which they mean to reward and vice versa, or fail to give feedback, and so on.

The job of the process consultant is to help the organization to solve its own problems by making it *aware of organizational processes,* of the consequences of these processes, and of the mechanisms by which they can be changed. The process consultant helps the organization to learn from self-diagnosis and self-intervention. The ultimate concern of the process consultant is the organization's capacity to do for itself what he has done for it. Where the standard consultant is more concerned about passing on his knowledge, the process consultant is concerned about passing on his skills and values.

REFERENCES

Argyris, C. "Explorations in Consultant-Client Relationships." *Hum. Org.,* 1961, **20**, 121-133.

Bales, R. F. *Interaction process analysis.* Reading, Mass.: Addison-Wesley, 1950.

Beckhard, R. "The confrontation meeting." *Harv. Bus. Rev.,* 1967, **54**, 149-154.

Benne, K. D. and Sheats, P. "Functional roles of group members." *J. Soc. Iss.,* 1948, **2**, 42-47.

Birdwhistell, R. L. "Paralanguage: Twenty-five years after Sapir," in *Lectures on experimental psychiatry* (H. Brosin, ed.) Pittsburgh: University of Pittsburgh Press, 1961.

Blake, R. R. and Mouton, Jane S. "Reactions to intergroup competition under win-lose conditions." *Man. Sci.,* 1961, **7**, 420-435.

Bradford, L. P., Gibb, J. R. and Benne, K. D. (eds). *"T-group theory and laboratory method."* New York: Wiley, 1964.

Carter, L., Haythorn, W., Meirowitz, B. and Lanzetta, J. "A note on a new technique of interaction recording." *J. Abn. Soc. Psych.,* 1951, **46**, 258-260.

Chapple, E. D. "Measuring human relations: An introduction to the study of interaction of individuals." *Gen. Psych. Mono.,* 1940, **22**, 3-147.

Daccord, J. E. "Management consultants: A study of the relationship between effectiveness and several personal characteristics." Unpublished Master's thesis, Sloan School of Management, M.I.T., 1967.

Dalton, M. *Men who manage.* New York: Wiley, 1959.

Daniel, D. R. "Reorganizing for results." *Harv. Bus. Rev.,* 1966, **44**, 96-104.

Hall, E. T. *The silent language.* New York: Doubleday, 1959.

Luft, J. "The Johari window." *Hum. Rel. Train. News,* 1961, **5**, 6-7.

Scheflen, A. E. "Quasi-courtship behavior in psychotherapy." *Psychiatry,* 1965, **28**, 245-55.

Schein, E. H. *Organizational psychology.* Englewood Cliffs, N.J.: Prentice-Hall, 1965.

Schein, E. H. and Bennis, W. G. *Personal and organizational change through group methods: the laboratory approach.* New York: Wiley, 1965.

Sherif, M., Harvey, O. J., White, B. J., Hood, W. R., and Sherif, C. W. *Intergroup Conflict and Cooperation,* Norman, Okla.: The University of Oklahoma Book Exchange, 1961.

Tannenbaum, R. and Schmidt, W. H. "How to choose a leadership pattern." *Harv. Bus. Rev.,* 1958, **36**, 95-101.

Taylor, F. W. *Scientific management.* New York: Harper & Bros., 1947.

Tilles, S. "Understanding the consultant's role." *Harv. Bus. Rev.,* 1961, **39**, 87-99.

White, R. and Lippitt, R. "Leader behavior and member reaction in three social climates," in *Group Dynamics* (D. Cartwright and A. Zander, eds.) White Plains, N.Y.: Row Peterson, 1953.

APPENDIX
SAMPLE THEORY MEMOS

MEMO I   SOME COMMENTS ON INTERNAL AUDITING
AND CONTROL PROGRAMS

A. *Some Ideas Why Internal Auditing Is Seen As Nonhelpful or As a Source of Tension:*

1. Auditors often feel primary loyalty to auditing group rather than company as a whole; they tend, at times, to feel themselves outside of the organization. Managers, on the other hand, feel primary loyalty to organization.

2. Auditors are typically rewarded for finding things wrong, less so for helping people get their work done. Managers, on the other hand, are rewarded for getting the job done, whether things were wrong or not.

3. Auditors tend to be (a) *perfectionists,* and (b) focused on *particular* problems in depth. Managers, on the other hand, tend to be (a) *"satisficers"* rather than maximizers (they tend to look for workable rather than perfect or ideal solutions), and (b) *generalists,* focusing on getting many imperfect things to work together toward getting a job done, rather than perfecting any one part of the job.

4. The auditor's job tempts him to *evaluate* the line operation and to propose solutions. The manager, on the other hand, wants *descriptive* (nonevaluative) feedback and to design his own solutions.

B. *Some Possible Dysfunctional Consequences of Tension between Line Organization and Auditing Function:*

1. Members of the line organization tend to pay attention to doing well, primarily in those areas which the auditor measures, whether those are important to the organizational mission or not.

2. Members of the line organization put effort into hiding problems and imperfections.

3. Management tends to use information about their subordinates in an unintentionally punishing way by immediate inquiries which gives subordinates the feeling of having the boss on their back even while they are already correcting the problem.

4. Members of the line organization are tempted to falsify and distort information to avoid punishment for being "found out," and to avoid having their boss "swoop down" on them.

5. *Detailed* information gathered by the auditing function tends to be passed too far up the line both in the auditing function and the line organization, making information available to people who are too far removed from the problem to know how to evaluate the information.

C. *Some Tentative Principles for the Handling of Auditing:*

1. *Line involvement:* The more the line organization is involved actively in decisions concerning (a) which areas of performance are to be audited, and (b) how the information is to be gathered and to whom it is to be given, the more helpful and effective the auditing function will be.

2. *Horizontal rather than vertical reporting:* The more the auditing information is made available, *first* to the man with the problem (horizontal reporting), then to his immediate boss only if the problem is not corrected, and then only to higher levels in either the line or the auditing group if the problem is still not corrected, the more likely it is that auditing will be effective (because line organizations will be less motivated to hide or falsify information and less likely to feel punished).

3. *Reward for helping rather than policing:* The more the managers in the auditing group reward their subordinates for being *helpful* (based on whether they are being perceived as helpful by the line) rather than being efficient in finding problem areas, the more effective

will be the auditing function.* (*Auditing people tend to be undertrained in how to use audit information in a helpful way; an appropriate reward system should be bolstered by training in how to give help.)

4. *Useful feedback:* The more the auditing information is *relevant* to important operational problems, *timely* in being fed back as soon after problem discovery as possible, and *descriptive* rather than evaluative, the more useful it will be to the line organization.

MEMO II   ORGANIZATION

1. The organization (any organization) can be thought of as having the following components:

   A. *Permanent Systems*
       Examples: product lines, product groups, manufacturing, finance, sales, executive committee

   B. *Temporary Systems*
       Examples: task forces, review committees, *ad hoc* problem-solving groups

   C. *Coordinating Systems* (may or may not be permanent)
       Examples: project groups which deliberately cut across product lines (e.g., standardization group); production engineering groups which coordinate between some product group and manufacturing; committees charged with functional responsibilities (e.g., engineering committee, salary committee, etc.)

This kind of classification focuses on the issue of whether you put any given function or group, like marketing, engineering, programming, etc., into a permanent, temporary, or coordinating role.

   The other point about the classification is the identification of weakness in the product line organization as the permanent system, and then the strengthening of the total organization by building appropriate temporary and coordinating systems to offset the weaknesses. For example, if lack of standardization is one of the weaknesses of the product line organization, you build special groups to worry about this, *but they can be temporary groups.*

The basic long-range question, then, is what kind of temporary and/or coordinating systems you need in order to make the product line organization work well.

MEMO III   EROSION OF RATIONALITY: ONE HAZARD
OF INTERNAL COMPETITION ON PRODUCT PLANNING

1.   One major alleged gain of competition is that it increases motivation to win. There is nothing in the ethic of competition, however, that guarantees rationality or concern for high quality (unless you can assume that you need rationality and quality in order to win, an assumption which is often untenable).

2.   A second major alleged gain of competition is that several independent problem-solvers may produce better solutions than those same problem-solvers working together.

3.   A major hazard of competition is that, in the desire to win for one's product, one may begin to exaggerate the virtues of one's own product and exaggerate the weaknesses of the competing product. If two or more competitors each begin this process of subtle distortion, it becomes harder and harder to determine the true strengths and weaknesses of each product.

4.   A second major hazard of competition is that in the process of selling one's own product solution one becomes emotionally committed to it. This commitment is one reason for the tendency to exaggerate (mentioned above). A further problem with commitment and loyalty based on competition is that it creates an attack-defense type of interaction. One is either selling, advocating, or defending. These types of interaction do not necessarily lead to effective problem-solving because they force both advocate and defender to play up only the good things in his project and

to try to hide the weaknesses. In other words, a debate does not encourage true, open communication. Yet can you solve problems rationally without true, open communications?

5. If during the process of competition one or more parties become personally threatened (i.e., their own job is threatened by the product decision), the danger arises that the inter*product* competition becomes an inter*personal* competition. If this happens, it becomes harder to make a rational product decision because it implies rejecting one *person*, not merely one *plan*. The issue is not whether this is actually true, but whether or not the participants *feel it to be true*.

6. Once competition becomes inter*personal*, participants increasingly become motivated to play politics and win by behind-the-scenes lobbying, undercutting the adversary, hiding information, making the other person look bad, etc. Once competition gets to this stage, it is very hard to undo, to get people to work together collaboratively.

7. How can these negative features be avoided while still gaining the advantages of competition?

A. *Be aware* of the hazards.

B. *Think through* at what point to switch from competition to collaboration *before* the competitive process has undermined rationality.

C. *Agree beforehand* at what point you will switch from competition to collaboration. Don't wait until you see the negative symptoms. By that time it may already be too late.

D. *Make sure everyone knows the ground rules and is willing to play the game that way.*

E. *Keep checking people's feelings,* as to whether they are beginning to feel threatened or not. *Build this kind of checking into meetings.* Don't let it become merely "conversation around the water-cooler."

F. *Learn to be flexible;* be able to switch back and forth from competition to collaboration and use each strategy when appropriate.